CRY BLOODY MURDER

CRY
BLOODY
MURDER

A Tale of Tainted Blood

———

Elaine DePrince

RANDOM HOUSE

NEW YORK

Library of Congress Cataloging-in-Publication Data

DePrince, Elaine.
Cry bloody murder: a tale of tainted blood/Elaine DePrince.
p.   cm.
Includes bibliographical references (p.   ).
ISBN 0-679-45676-7
1. DePrince, Elaine.   2. AIDS (Disease)–United States–Biography.
3. Hemophiliacs–United States–Biography.   4. Mothers–United
States–Biography.   5. Blood–Transfusion–Complications–United
States.   6. AIDS (Disease)–Transmission–United States.   I. Title.
RC607.A26D468   1997
362.1′969792′0092–dc21
[B]   96-29970

Random House website address: http://www.randomhouse.com/

Printed in the United States of America on acid-free paper

24689753

FIRST EDITION

Book design by Carole Lowenstein

To
Mike and Cubby,
whose
wisdom comforted me,
whose
courage inspired me,
whose
deaths motivated the writing of this book

CONTENTS

INTRODUCTION

On a mild, sunny April morning in 1994, I received a telephone call from a funeral director. The ashes of my fifteen-year-old son were ready to be picked up. When I put down the phone, I thought about the box containing Michael's remains. I knew that it would weigh no more than six or seven pounds. Sometime in late June my husband and I would walk along the Appalachian Trail in Virginia, carrying the box to a peaceful mountaintop. We would gently scatter handfuls of ashes among the wildflowers, and I knew exactly how the ashes would feel against our fingers—rough and pebbly. I knew exactly how the meadow would look. Mauve blossoms of milkweed and sunny yellow common mullein would just be awakening. There would be lots of red columbine, with its clappers of yellow stamens. Butterflies and fritillaries would be drifting about, celebrating life.

I knew all of this, and I knew how we would feel as we hiked back to our campsite, weeping along the way. I knew this because I had experienced it before. This was the second child of mine whose ashes I would leave upon that mountain. Michael's ashes would mingle with those of his brother, eleven-year-old Cubby. I had left Cubby's ashes there the year before.

As I think of this, I cannot repress my sorrow, my pain, and my rage. My sons were infected with HIV and died of AIDS because they used a blood product approved by the Food and Drug Administration. The FDA failed my children. The blood-banking industry failed them. Government agencies failed them. The law failed them.

My sons had hemophilia, but what happened to them also happened to thousands of people who didn't have hemophilia. What happened to my sons happened to people who were born hale and hearty and who required a blood transfusion because they had been in an accident or had elective surgery. Anyone can find himself on the receiving end of a stranger's blood.

––––––––

In 1966, the first license to market a clotting factor to treat hemophilia was granted by the Food and Drug Administration. By 1983, the median life span of a hemophiliac had risen from forty years to fifty-seven, with the greatest reduction in fatalities occurring in children. During this period, however, thousands of hemophiliacs contracted various types of hepatitis from the clotting factor they were now taking to treat routine bleeding episodes. Since hepatitis and other known blood-borne viruses seemed a small price to pay to avoid bleeding to death, hemophiliacs were willing to gamble with odds that they believed were stacked in their favor. But this didn't take into account the incipient AIDS epidemic. By 1988, more than half the hemophiliacs in the United States were infected with HIV. By 1994, the median life span of a hemophiliac was back to what it had been in 1966.

The first three documented transfusion-related AIDS cases in this country involved hemophiliacs, each of whom regularly received a plasma product made from blood given by thousands of donors. Blood-banking and government regulatory agencies were slow to respond to these cases, even when the Centers for Disease Control recommended action. Stricter donor guidelines, more adequate donor-blood testing, and improved viral-inactivation processes were not expediently initiated.

The likelihood of another contamination of our blood supply by a virus even more devastating than HIV cannot be ignored. Even now the available blood is not totally free of commonplace transfusion-transmitted viruses for which screening programs exist. The ill effects of some of the most common blood-borne viruses can range from mild clinical illness to such devastating destruction as liver failure, bone marrow failure, blindness, massive hemorrhage, fatal encephalitis, irreversible organ damage, lymphoma, leukemia, or degenerative neurological disorders. There are also, of course, many viruses for which blood is not tested—not necessarily because testing is expensive, but simply because in some cases a reliable test is either unavailable or undependable.

When one is aware of the extraordinary pain suffered by hemophiliacs on a regular basis, one is better able to understand why they so readily accepted, often without question, a treatment that relieved their suffering and reduced crippling but included the possible transmission of potentially deadly viruses. Over the years, hemophiliacs have been treated with egg whites, bee stings, peanuts, cigarette smoke, lime, hydrogen peroxide, gelatin, and female hormones. When a genuinely effective, convenient treatment for hemophilia was finally developed, it was possible for manufacturers of the treatment to keep a virally contaminated product on the market long after doing so was justified. They called it "benefit versus risk." But the risk needn't have existed. The tragedy that felled my sons was not an act of God. It was avoidable. And if we become informed, alert, and questioning consumers in the matter of medical treatment, perhaps we can avoid something similar happening in the future. It is my hope that knowing our story will help others protect themselves.

From the time clotting-factor concentrate was first licensed in the 1960s to the present, manufacturers often changed the names of their companies, reincorporated, or merged with other companies. In telling this story, I discovered that I was left with a hodgepodge of names that varied from year to year for each corporation, its subsidiaries, and its divisions. To simplify things, I refer to these corporations as Alpha, Armour, Baxter, and Bayer. This is how they are designated in class-action documents filed in the U.S. District Court for the Northern District of Illinois. The other corporate names of these companies or their subsidiaries and divisions are used only if they are part of a document, used in a quotation or in a paraphrase of a quotation, or reference is made to them by a party other than the author.

CRY BLOODY MURDER

CHAPTER 1

——— ◊ ———

Love of Blood

"Mommy, Mommy—"

I spring instantly awake. Whose voice is that? Which room is it coming from?

"Please, Mommy!"

It's Cubby, my four-year-old. I know before I get to his room that it will be his knee. It is a mess of torn cartilage and ragged bone, and he suffers from frequent hemorrhages.

Cubby's knee is the size of a cantaloupe. It is red and hot, and he moans pathetically when I try to pick him up. Charles, my husband, appears in the doorway. "Do you want me to carry him down?" he asks.

Charles gently places Cubby on the living room sofa while I prepare an infusion of factor VIII, a clotting substance. Cubby's veins are tiny and difficult to locate, so I pray hard for a successful first stick. The needle hits its target, and I begin to push the clotting factor through the syringe.

When I finish with the injection, I prepare a cup of warm milk for Cubby and give him Tylenol with Codeine. Last of all, I pack three bags of frozen peas around his knee. Bags of peas are much more flexible than bags of ice cubes.

I sit on a chair holding Cubby's hand. Finally he drifts off to sleep, poor baby. I kiss his pale, tear-streaked face and settle down at the kitchen table with a novel and a cup of coffee, but I can't concentrate on my book. I keep wondering what I can do to prevent Cubby's knee joint from hemorrhaging three times a week.

———————

Hemophilia is an ancient disease. A fifth-century text in the Talmud refers to "a familial bleeding disorder . . . that led to a rabbinic decree relating to circumcision." The decree exempted any Jewish male baby from circumcision if two previous sons of his mother or sons of his mother's sister hemorrhaged when circumcised. Hemophilia was the inherited scourge of a number of the royal families of Europe, to whom the disease was passed through marriages with the daughters of Queen Victoria. One of the most famous of the royal hemophiliacs was young Alexis, the only son of Czar Nicholas II of Russia.

Hemophilia was proposed as a name for the disease in a British medical treatise in 1828. The word means "love of blood," though no phrase could less accurately describe what a hemophiliac feels. He dreads the excruciating pain caused by blood leaking drop by pulsing drop into joints, muscles, and internal organs. There was a kind of prescience in this choice of a name, however, for it was finally the blood of human donors that offered victims of hemophilia a promise of relief from pain and the possibility of a normal life.

Before modern methods to treat hemophilia were devised, many attempts to control hemorrhaging had been made. The Romanovs relied on Rasputin, who taught the czarevitch self-hypnosis. Through hypnosis, Alexis experienced some release from his pain and even had a little control over his hemorrhaging (thus strengthening the position of Rasputin in the czar's household).

———————

Again Cubby's knee is hot, swollen and throbbingly painful. Again he is lying on the sofa. He is five years old. Despite the bags of frozen peas packed around his knee, he is sweating. Runnels of perspiration leave paths down his forehead. I tell him about Rasputin and self-hypnosis. Cubby agrees to give it a try.

Taking ideas from a book on meditation, I begin to drone in a calm, soothing voice: "You are sitting in a beautiful green field of blossoming clover. The breezes are sifting through your hair. You are totally relaxed from the tips of your toes to the top of your head. Small, furry, gentle rabbitlike creatures come hopping across the field. They stop before you. You give each one a tiny handful of your pain. The line of creatures seems to reach to the horizon as each creature stops to collect a piece of Cubby-pain."

With eyes closed, Cubby has relaxed. As I pause for a breath, his eyes pop open. "Come on, Mommy, tell me more. I don't feel hypnotized, but this is a pretty good story. Where do the rabbits take the pain? What happens next?"

I look at Cubby's earnest face and laugh. "Oh, Cubs, maybe that's what hypnosis is all about—getting you to think about something else. I wonder how Rasputin did it?" As Cubby looks at me expectantly, I continue the hypnosis exercise gone awry. At least Cubby will be entertained and distracted—and he has stopped sweating.

———

Although scientists had suspected by the early nineteenth century that a hemophiliac's blood was missing something that is present in the blood of nonbleeders, it was only in the twentieth century that the disease unfolded its secrets.

Blood is made up of a solid part and a liquid part. The solid part is composed of red blood cells, white cells, and platelets, each with their respective function of transporting oxygen, fighting infection, and aiding coagulation. The tiny oval or circular platelets are sticky and have a tendency to clump together at the site of an injury. Since they are necessary for clot formation, early-twentieth-century scientists mistakenly assumed that they are involved in hemophilia. But in the late 1930s, evidence began to link hemophilia to a defect in the plasma, the liquid portion of blood.

Plasma is composed of proteins, salts, sugars, and water. Fourteen different plasma proteins have been found to effect clotting. These are referred to as clotting factors. Seventeen recognized disorders (coagulopathies) result from deficiencies of these clotting factors.

Several of the deficiencies are asymptomatic. Some cause mild problems. Others are more severe, and still others create problems of variable degrees in the same patient at different times. Most coagulopathies are hereditary. The three most common of these are von Willebrand disease, hemophilia A, and the relatively rarer hemophilia B.

Just days after I had delivered my first baby, my son Adam, our pediatrician was standing in the middle of my hospital room in a bloody gown, his face red and contorted with rage. "Why didn't you tell me there was hemophilia in your family? That baby bled like a stuck pig when I circumcised him!"

Shocked, I stammered that I didn't know what he was talking about–although I did have haunting memories of my mother hemorrhaging so badly at the birth of my younger brother that she went into cardiac arrest. And both my younger brother and I had experienced bruising and joint pain significant enough to exclude us from some childhood activities.

The pediatrician ordered a series of blood tests that indicated that Adam had neither hemophilia A nor hemophilia B. There was no mention of von Willebrand disease. I assume the pediatrician either didn't know or neglected to tell me that the test results could simply have been reflecting the fact that clotting-factor levels are falsely high in newborns. Women produce extraordinarily high levels of the clotting factors in late pregnancy–even women who suffer from coagulopathies–and these high levels are temporarily passed on to the neonate, which can disguise von Willebrand disease.

When my second son, Erik, was born a year later, the pediatrician was concerned about his pallor and projectile vomiting. I was concerned about the enormous lump on his head and the fact that the left side of his face drooped. He came home when he was eight days old, droopy faced and still vomiting. I have no doubt that if the kind of imaging techniques that are available now had been in use then, they would have detected intracranial bleeding.

Erik had frequent streptococcus infections. His joints swelled. He was anemic. A doctor suggested that Erik's joint problem and anemia were related to the strep infections and recommended a tonsillectomy. I was apprehensive about the surgery because my sons and I had experienced far too many episodes of unexplained hemorrhaging. We apparently had some type of coagulopathy, but it remained undiagnosed. As a precaution against hemorrhaging, a hematologist scheduled an Ivy bleeding-time test for Erik on the afternoon before the surgery.

An abnormal Ivy bleeding time contraindicates surgery. The test is performed by using a blood-pressure cuff as a tourniquet and making two very tiny incisions on the inside of the patient's forearm. Bleeding from the site of the incisions is observed, and the length of time between the start of bleeding and the formation of a clot is measured.

Erik's Ivy bleeding time fell within the normal range of three to eight minutes, so his surgery proceeded as scheduled. On tonsillectomy day, the surgeon, a physician I'd known for years, sensed my apprehension, and before he wheeled Erik into the operating room, he told me, "Ahh, don't worry. I'll have him out in forty minutes."

I nervously tried to read in the waiting room while a little boy who was scheduled to have a myringotomy, a minor operation in which minuscule tubes are placed in the eardrum, badgered his mother. He was anxious, and his constant refrain of "Mom, what's taking Dr. Pat so long?" began to fray my nerves further because I suspected that something *was* wrong. It didn't help that the little boy's mother kept saying things like "Don't worry; the doctor is probably just having a problem with the little boy who went in before you. He was having a more serious operation than yours." Finally I asked her to stop. It was my little boy who was in there so long.

After three hours, Dr. Pat came plowing through the doors, looking upset. "I don't know what it is that's wrong with your son," he said to me, "but I suggest that you find a place to take him for a diagnosis before he bleeds to death some day. I didn't think that I was ever going to stop the bleeding. I had to put stitches in his throat."

Eventually I learned that we have von Willebrand disease, a bleeding disorder named for Dr. Erik Adolph von Willebrand, the Finnish physician who first identified it. Erik had passed the Ivy bleeding-time test before his tonsillectomy because the clotting-factor level in people with von Willebrand disease fluctuates. Erik's test demonstrated only that he did not suffer from prolonged bleeding during the afternoon on which the test was performed. It could not predict that his clotting-factor level would drop by the next morning, just at the wrong time.

Our symptoms challenge the textbook description of von Willebrand disease. We are supposed to suffer from prolonged bleeding of the mucous membranes and possibly hemorrhages in organs. We do that, but we also bleed into our muscles and joints, something that the books tell us we should not be doing. As I meet more and more people with von Willebrand disease, I discover that the books are not always right and that we are not so unusual.

For me, the diagnosis put a label on years of mysterious bruises and recurring joint and muscle injuries. I don't have rheumatoid arthritis or fragile blood vessels. I don't have a vitamin C deficiency. There is a very good reason why, when I was a child, my skinned knees seemed to bleed forever. I have a genetic disorder that I passed on to my sons—and that they can pass on to their children.

Each cell of the human body has twenty-three pairs of chromosomes. One of these pairs is the sex chromosomes, the X and Y chromosomes. The other twenty-two pairs are referred to as autosomes. Von Willebrand disease is the result of a defect on chromosome 12, one of the autosomes, and is inherited by males and females with equal frequency. This defect affects the levels of von Willebrand factor, a protein in the blood that helps platelets plug a leaking blood vessel wall by carrying factor VIII (another blood protein vital to coagulation) to the site of an injury. The abnormal clotting of people with von Willebrand disease is caused primarily by a deficiency of the von Willebrand factor.

The inheritance of both hemophilia A and hemophilia B is sex-linked. That is, the defects that cause these conditions are carried on the X chromosome. (In a female, there are two X chromosomes, and in a male there are one X chromosome and one Y chromosome. When an egg cell is fertilized, the female contributes one of its Xs, and the male contributes either its X or its Y. If the cell receives two Xs, it will be female; if it receives an X and a Y, it will be male.) In hemophilia, as in von Willebrand disease, a chromosomal defect results in the insufficient production of certain clotting factors. Hemophilia A is caused by a deficiency of factor VIII, while hemophilia B is caused by a deficiency of factor IX, which is yet another protein necessary for coagulation.

A female child (two X chromosomes) born to a carrier mother (one defective X, one normal X) and a nonhemophilic father (one normal X, one normal Y) has a fifty-fifty chance of receiving her mother's defective chromosome. If she does receive it, she, too, will be a carrier. A daughter of a hemophilic male will always be a carrier, because she will inherit her father's defective X chromosome. Since the carrier female's normal X chromosome compensates for the defective chromosome, the female carrier is not a hemophiliac, though some females are symptomatic for mild hemophilia. Only in the rare case of genetic mutation or in the case of a female child of a hemophilic father and a carrier mother who receives both her mother's and father's defective X chromosomes is a female a moderate or severe hemophiliac.

A male child (one X chromosome, one Y chromosome) born to a carrier mother also has a fifty-fifty chance of receiving his mother's defective X chromosome. His second chromosome is a Y, which plays no role in blood clotting. If he receives the defective X chromosome, he will have hemophilia, for he will have no way of compensating.

Nonetheless, approximately one-third of hemophiliacs have no family history of the disease. Their hemophilia is caused by a genetic mutation of one of their mother's X chromosomes. Though exact statistics are not available for patients with von Willebrand disease, their defect may also appear for the first time in a patient with no family history of the disease. Hemophilia A occurs in one in every ten thousand male births. Hemophilia B occurs in one in one hundred thousand male births. Von Willebrand disease is estimated to occur in approximately 1 to 2 percent of the population. Because it is most common in its mildest form, it can be overlooked until trauma or surgery is complicated by unexpected hemorrhaging that requires a transfusion. Many von Willebrand patients never experience the automobile accident or operation that would lead to a diagnosis.

Clotting-factor deficiencies cannot be fully appreciated without an understanding of the realities of life with a bleeding disorder. Until recently, the major cause of death among hemophiliacs was hemorrhaging. Bleeding in a hemophiliac can be either trauma induced or spontaneous (with no provoking injury). Some severe hemophiliacs hemorrhage only once a month. Others hemorrhage as often as three or more times a week. Blood loss weakens the hemophiliac by causing persistent anemia and damage to organs, joints, and muscles. Certain bleeding episodes are life threatening.

An intracranial hemorrhage can occur as a result of a minor bump on the head. Considering the frequency with which babies fall, it takes little imagination to recognize the risk to young hemophiliacs who are just learning to toddle about. An untreated hemophiliac with intracranial hemorrhaging may not die, but he is likely to go blind, become paralyzed, or have severe learning disabilities. Abdominal hemorrhages are horribly painful and extremely dangerous. Massive blood loss and shock can rapidly result from an abdominal hemorrhage. Some abdominal hemorrhages can occur within a small organ, destroying it.

———

"That lasagna gave me gas, Mom."

Instantly suspicious, I ask Erik, who is now thirteen, "Are you sure you didn't get hurt while you were riding your bike tonight?"

"Sure I'm sure," Erik insists as he raises his T-shirt to show me his torso. "See, Mom, no bruises." Assured, I offer him a cup of warm milk, my stopgap treatment for everything.

Erik asks to sleep in Adam's room, because they want to watch a late movie together. Since it's summertime, I honor the request.

One minute I am sound asleep, and the next I am awakened by Adam, yelling incoherently at the foot of our bed. Charles and I sit up, stunned. I try to calm Adam down enough so that I can understand what he's saying.

"Help, oh God! Help. It's Erik. He's moaning and rolling around. I don't know if he's conscious." Charles and I bolt out of bed. As we approach Adam's bedroom, Erik begins to scream in agony.

If we call an ambulance, we'll probably have a twenty-minute wait, so we decide to drive Erik to the hospital around the corner. Erik isn't able to walk, and Adam, who at age fourteen is nearly six feet tall, carries his brother to our van. On the way to the hospital, Adam recalls that Erik was nearly knocked off his bicycle the night before by a friend. Erik remembers that he did slightly bump his upper abdomen, but just ever so slightly.

Once we are in the hospital, I give the emergency room physicians the telephone number of our hematologist. I explain to them that I think Erik is suffering from an internal hemorrhage. The emergency room staff treats me as though I were more than slightly deranged.

I am kept out of the emergency room while Erik is examined. Then I am invited in. When I am about a dozen paces from Erik's cubicle, he begins to scream. The emergency room physician tells me that Erik is putting on an act for me. Upon palpating Erik's abdomen, he is unable to detect a problem. He thinks Erik has gas.

I am horrified. I look at the physician and ask, "You palpated his abdomen after I told you that he has a bleeding disorder?"

The emergency room physician tells me to take Erik home. He's fine. The gas will pass. I refuse to do so until he gives Erik either fresh-frozen plasma or cryoprecipitate, products that will enable his blood to clot. The physician refuses to do this and refuses to telephone our hematologist in New York.

I insist that Erik be taken to another hospital, one that is a half hour away but has both a pediatric hematologist and a trauma unit. I threaten to sue, so the physician accedes to my wish.

The ambulance crew asks whether Erik is stable. The emergency room physician claims that he is—he only has gas. Erik is driven away in the ambulance. Adam and I follow in the van.

When I arrive at the second hospital, the ambulance crew is cursing. They are telling me that the doctor at the first hospital lied to them. Erik wasn't stable. He vomited all over them, and his blood pressure went crazy.

At the second hospital, Erik is sent for an immediate CT scan. The results show that he is hemorrhaging into his pancreas. A surgeon is summoned. Erik eventually receives the appropriate blood product. Fourteen hours after his admission to the hospital, intravenous morphine has not deadened the pain enough to keep him from yelling and moaning.

Erik recovers from the pancreas hemorrhage with his insulin production intact. I am told he was lucky. He could have developed diabetes or died.

With the introduction of more effective treatment protocols in the mid- to late 1960s, the number of deaths among hemophiliacs due to severe internal hemorrhaging decreased precipitously. Bleeds are still painful, but in most cases they are controllable. Injuries to the head, abdomen, and face or neck can still prove fatal, but such fatalities occur far less often in 1995 than they did in 1955. Nonetheless, early bleeds are sometimes difficult to recognize, and pain is still a frequent companion throughout the life of a hemophiliac.

Even with optimal treatment, something as simple as an injection of an anesthetic by a dentist in preparation for drilling a tooth and filling a cavity can create complications. Bleeding occurs internally at the site of the injection, and this can cause swelling in the throat and can eventually block the air from passing through the trachea, causing the patient to suffocate. It was not unusual for a child born in an age when no treatment was available to die from something as banal as a nosebleed.

In the past, each time a hemophiliac hemorrhaged into a joint, it filled with huge quantities of blood. Damage was caused by the irritating effects of iron in the blood's hemoglobin and by nature's way of removing this irritation. That is, the body produces enzymes that digest the blood left behind after a bleed, but the enzymes also digest cartilage and bone. So each time the enzymes went to work after a bleed, the joint would be damaged further. Eventually the cushion of cartilage could be completely dissolved and the bone worn or chipped.

These days, blood seldom has an opportunity to fill a joint. Hemorrhages can be stopped early because treatment is quick, efficient, and often takes place in the home. But even today it would be foolhardy to underrate the life-threatening potential of hemophilia or its ability to maim. Without appropriate, adequate, and timely treatment, a person with hemophilia is no better off than the czarevitch Alexis was in the early years of the twentieth century.

CHAPTER 2

The Last Golden Moment

Since von Willebrand disease was first documented in 1926 but not understood until the mid-1950s, it is not surprising that my family didn't know why I was crying on the day in 1950 that is memorialized by an old black-and-white photograph. There I stand, in front of my grandmother's porch—a tiny, fair-haired, sad-faced little girl with her left arm and shoulder in an awkward position. I was three years old, and I can still remember accusing my well-meaning teenage aunts of pulling my shoulder out of its socket. They were befuddled and upset. All they had done was take me for a walk, and, to my delight, they swung me by the arms over every curbside puddle.

That is the first "bleed" that I can remember, though on Tuesday, June 16, 1948, my mother had unknowingly documented one of my earliest bleeds. She wrote in my baby book that "Baby Elaine walked to Mother without help, but then she fell and sprained her wrist, so she didn't walk any more until she was twelve months old." Nearly a half century passed before I learned from an orthopedist that it is anatomically impossible for a ten-month-old baby to sprain her wrist.

My childhood was plagued by "bad ankles" that left me a playground outcast. In the 1950s, schoolgirls jumped rope, and double

Dutch was the rage. The most popular girls were the best jumpers. I was dreadfully clumsy at this, and after just two or three jumps the throbbing ankle pain would begin.

My earliest and most pervasive memory, one that dates back to my first vestiges of consciousness, does not involve painful joints. It is my memory of the "draft." My mother and grandmother would say, "Elaine, close the door. You don't want to let in a draft." Long before I learned that the draft to which they referred was a current of chilly air, I thought of it as the cloud that would often overwhelm me. I would be playing with my dolls or coloring when suddenly the draft would engulf me. I would be lost in a drifting world. The draft terrified me.

As I grew older, I understood that when the draft came, I lost time. When I was a teenager, the draft was given a new name—epilepsy. Because I can recall the draft being a part of my life from the beginning, and my mother can recall my long moments of stillness dating back to my babyhood, the epilepsy more than likely resulted from undiagnosed intracranial bleeding at the time of my birth.

I entered adulthood with undiagnosed von Willebrand disease, yet I graduated from college, studied for a master's degree, and taught school. Eventually I married and unknowingly passed von Willebrand disease on to Adam and Erik. Their childhoods were very much like mine. They had unusual episodes of bleeding. Adam was hospitalized at the age of two with gastrointestinal bleeding. Erik suffered a bad "sprain" of his hip when he was a year old. Both boys suffered from numerous sprained ankles, and Erik regularly sprained his hips, elbows, shoulders, fingers, and knees as well.

With our family's history, my husband and I felt equipped to handle another child with a bleeding disorder, so when a baby with hemophilia A became available for adoption, we opened our home and hearts to Michael-Noah, a child with a mouthful of a name because Charles and I couldn't agree on which name to give him. We eventually called him Mikey, spelled *M-i-k-e,* because as a preschooler he refused to print his full name. Actually, it didn't really matter to Mike what we called him. He couldn't hear us. He was deaf. He also had a cleft lip and palate. None of these conditions was related to his hemophilia.

When Mike was a little boy, his hemophilia was far easier to deal with than either his deafness or the complications of his cleft palate. If he had a bleed, I treated him with factor VIII concentrate, which we stored at home. It was freeze-dried and resembled powdered milk. The tiny glass factor VIII bottles were packaged along with bottles containing approximately ten to thirty milliliters of sterile water. With a two-way needle, I transferred the sterile water into the factor VIII bottle, then rolled the bottle gently between my palms in order to mix the solution thoroughly. Then I drew the solution into a syringe and injected it into Mike's vein with a twenty-five-gauge butterfly-shaped infusion needle.

At first, Mike screamed and carried on something awful every time he needed an infusion. But it didn't take long for me to realize that he objected more to being held down than he did to the needle, and by the time he was three years old, he would open the refrigerator, take out a box of factor VIII, and hand it to me if he had a bleed.

Some early photographs of Mike show him wearing a protective helmet, hearing aid, glasses, and short leg braces. The first three of these items usually disappeared the second my back was turned. He flushed his hearing aids down the toilet twice and fed them to the dog once. He usually buried his glasses in the sandbox, but one summer he found a better, more permanent place to dispose of them. Charles and I had traveled to Canada with Adam, Erik, and Mike, and we took a boat to an island off the coast of the Gaspé Peninsula and hiked to an Arctic bird preserve. As we watched the ritual behaviors of millions of gannets, Mike threw his glasses over a cliff and into the Gulf of St. Lawrence. Charles caught the helmet as it followed the glasses. We didn't have to worry about the hearing aid. That had already disappeared into our campground's septic system.

Mike liked his metal leg braces, which had been prescribed to support his hemorrhage-weakened ankles. He would thunder over the floors, pounding his feet as hard as he could. He enjoyed the vibrations he produced, but they gave me a headache. When I discovered that Mike could run away from me just as quickly without his braces as with them, we put the noisy things away for good, but he would dig them out of the closet and insist on wearing them. Then we bought him sneakers just like his big brother Erik's, and he abandoned the braces.

By the time Mike was five years old, he had hiked portions of the Appalachian Trail from Tennessee to Maine. He had followed me on expeditions to photograph moose and had climbed Cannon Mountain in the White Mountains of New Hampshire. Hiking was a more carefree activity for Mike than it was for Adam, Erik, or me. Mike's factor VIII for treating hemophilia was just a backpack away. Treatment on the trail took less than ten minutes. An injury to me or to my two oldest sons meant a trip to the hospital for fresh-frozen plasma or cryoprecipitate, which were needed to stop the bleeding caused by our von Willebrand disease.

Charles and I thought that life couldn't be more perfect than it was in November 1985. We had three happy boys. Charles was nearing the end of six years' work toward his M.B.A. I finally had time to write and sell stories to children's magazines. I thought about all this the week of Thanksgiving, when I drove to Trenton, New Jersey, for a meeting with the director of the New Jersey Division of Youth and Family Services, to discuss the problems of families with adopted children with special needs. At the end of the meeting, I was asked whether I would be willing to take two more little boys. I thought this was a joke and put the request out of my mind.

A month later, at Christmastime, I was again asked whether I would consider taking two more little boys with hemophilia. "I've been through potty training enough times, and I'm not ready to deal with rebellious teenagers," I answered—I thought facetiously—"so if you tell me that they're four and five years old, you've got a deal." They were four and five years old. They came to us in January with names that were more appropriate for middle-aged men, so we nicknamed them Teddy and Cubby, because they reminded us of a pair of bear cubs.

Teddy and Cubby had experienced neglect, abuse, and emotional deprivation. Teddy arrived with new stitches in his head. He wasn't in the door five minutes before I was telephoning the hemophilia center for information about his injury. The poor child–not only was he terrified of living with a new family, but his new mother almost immediately stuck a needle into his vein. He must have suffered terribly from untreated hemorrhages before he came to us, for rather than object to the treatment, he grilled me curiously about the procedure and wanted to know whether bleeds could have been treated at home this way when he was a baby. When I answered yes, he told me, "Then I'm going to pretend I just got born, and I'm going to call you Mommy."

I had no sooner lifted Teddy off the kitchen table than I noticed Cubby dragging his left leg. His knee was so swollen that I couldn't raise his pant leg over it. Again I placed a blanket on the kitchen table and lifted Cubby up for an infusion of factor VIII. Though I tried to explain the concept of home care to these two little boys, it was years before they stopped telling their friends that their mommy was a nurse.

Teddy and Cubby had been with us a short while when the family's orthopedic surgeon prescribed braces for Cubby's and Adam's left knees. Cubby had suffered severe damage to his knee as a result of having been stabbed with a stick when he was two years old. The injury and resulting hemorrhage were complicated by osteomyelitis, an infection in the bone. Cubby couldn't walk without hemorrhaging into the damaged knee. Twelve-year-old Adam had gone through a growth spurt that year and suffered a series of knee-joint bleeds as a result. A knee brace would stabilize the knee and limit the range of motion for several months.

The knee braces provided a bonding experience for the boys. Cubby was convinced that both he and Adam had problems with their left knees because they were brothers. He was proud of having crutches like Adam's, although Adam's were fitted to a strapping boy nearly six feet tall, and Cubby's fit his tiny, thirty-inch frame. Wherever Adam leaned his crutches, Cubby would place his next to them.

Eventually Cubby convinced himself that he even looked like Adam, although both he and Teddy had been born to Puerto Rican parents, and Cubby looked like a boy from India. During the first week of first grade, Cubby was taken out of class for a session with a physical therapist, who commented that he had another DePrince on his schedule, an Adam DePrince. Bubbling with enthusiasm, brown-skinned, black-haired Cubby said, "That's my big brother, and you'll have no trouble finding him, because he looks exactly like me."

That afternoon the physical therapist roamed the high school in search of a teenager named Adam DePrince with brown skin and black hair, who was supposed to meet him in the adaptive-physical-education room. The gym teacher told the physical therapist that Adam DePrince was already there, but the only person in the room was a blue-eyed, freckled-faced boy with curly sandy-brown hair. Finally the baffled physical therapist asked the freckled boy, "Have you seen an Indian boy named Adam DePrince?" Adam laughed and said, "I guess you must have met my brother Cubby."

Life with three sons had been good, but life with five sons was even better. Initially I was concerned that Mike would feel jealous, but he was delighted to have two new playmates close to his age. If any jealousy existed, it was between Teddy and Cubby, who vied for the position of Mike's spokesperson and protector. No neighborhood child dared to pick on Mike with Cubby and Teddy around. Not that they would fight. They yelled. Their voices were so loud that I'd hear them a block away.

Five sons meant that being alone was a matter of choice for each child. Five sons meant that there was always something going on. Having five sons meant that Charles and I could sit and read novels on the beach while the younger boys spent endless hours building empires in the sand supervised by their older brothers. Having five sons with coagulopathies meant that rarely did one child sit alone recovering from a joint bleed, because the boys always seemed to hemorrhage in pairs.

Erik was the companion of choice of any of the younger children with a bleed. Being paired with Erik meant hours of art projects. He would draw spacecraft, jet planes, or cartoon strips for them to color. He and Cubby would plan the writing and illustration of a book, draw and color cartoons, develop a new board game and play it, or create a planet full of Play-Doh aliens.

Hemophilia care was so easy for the three children in our family who used factor VIII concentrate that I became determined to administer cryoprecipitate at home to treat Adam, Erik, and myself. After a lesson from our hemophilia nurse on the thawing and pooling of cryoprecipitate, I was ready for our first delivery of cryo from the Red Cross. It arrived at night, packed in dry ice. We quickly transferred bags of the frozen caramel-colored substance to our freezer and prepared for what would become a happy ritual known as making witches' brew.

Witches' brew resulted from dumping a box of dry ice into a trash can filled with water. When the dry ice came in contact with the water, billowing clouds of stage smoke were produced. The boys would take turns moaning like ghosts or cackling like witches while they recited the witches' lines from *Macbeth:* "Double, double toil and trouble . . ."

Perhaps we were, as one friend claimed, a family that when handed lemons, made lemonade. But we never thought of it that way. Hemophilia was a fact of life to be dealt with, not lamented. The children gave little thought to the significance of the cryo delivery. They took turns watching at the front door for the white van with the red cross in anticipation of the fun and frolic of making witches' brew.

The bond between the children continued to strengthen as a result of their shared experiences with bleeds and intravenous treatment at home. The differences between biological children and adopted children blurred and disappeared. Adam and Erik were biological siblings. Teddy and Cubby were biological siblings. Yet if someone asked any one of the boys, "How's your brother?" the answer would always be "Which one?" Years later, when I read the memoirs Cubby wrote before he died, I learned that this answer was not as ingenuous as it seemed. The boys thought of themselves as the five DePrince brothers. They resented it when an outsider had the effrontery to differentiate between adopted and nonadopted. Woe to the insensitive soul who made the mistake of asking, "Which brother is your *real* brother?"

I didn't realize just how strongly affected the smaller children were by the shared medical experiences until one day when I was giving myself an infusion of cryo to treat a shoulder-joint bleed. Cubby, who was about seven then, kissed my arm and said, "I know that I couldn't love a birth mother as much as I love you because she wouldn't need to get factor." I understood then that the closeness among siblings and between mother and children in our family was born not just of love but of empathy, a sentiment rarely felt by children for their parents.

I often worried that Charles might lose out because he did not have a bleeding disorder. But his normality became a source of concern to the children. Charles spent a lot of his spare time making minor household repairs, and occasionally he'd injure himself, usually by hammering his thumb. As he howled, clutching the mashed thumb and hopping around the room, Teddy or Cubby would sympathize, telling him, "Poor Daddy, if only you had hemophilia, Mommy could give you factor VIII, and you'd feel all better again."

Despite his sqeamishness over blood and needles and his utter inability to stick a vein, Charles was perfect for a family like us because he didn't have a macho bone in his body. He didn't measure the worth of his sons by their physical prowess. Charles admired his children for whatever skills they possessed: Adam for his genius with computers, Erik for his artistic flair, Teddy for his musical talent and his acting ability, Mike for his speed-reading, and Cubby for his precocious verbal abilities and his charisma.

Charles also had a knack for telling stories, especially scary ones and especially when we were around a campfire. Some were silly stories with no sense to them at all. One regular character was Sneaky Snake, who was always getting into trouble. Sneaky Snake stories were in such demand that Charles often tape-recorded them before he went away on a business trip, so that the children could hear the sound of his voice while he was away.

Charles and I filled our sons' summers with camping, hiking, backpacking, canoeing, and swimming. We filled their winters with sledding, ice-skating, and walks along the windy New Jersey seashore. The boys responded by acting like normal kids. They preferred to run rather than walk, climb trees rather than sit under them, and jump over something rather than walk around it. When they did these things, Charles and I issued the usual parental warnings and held our breaths. Amazingly, they survived.

When I look back on the childhood of our sons, I think of the summer of 1986 as the last golden moment. For most of our married life, Charles and I had wanted to visit Nova Scotia. Looking forward to a month's vacation, the seven of us pored over maps and guidebooks and decided on an itinerary. The boys wanted to see whales off the coast of Maine, watch the tides come in at the Bay of Fundy, hike the wild taiga of northern Nova Scotia's Cape Breton Island, search for moose in the north woods of Maine, and see the farmhouse in Vermont where Charles and I had lived as newlyweds.

The trip was magical from beginning to end. We bought tickets for a whale watch aboard a research vessel. Unlike the commercial whale-watch boats, ours stayed out until the sun set. In the afternoon, we sighted a humpback whale and her calf. I told Teddy and Cubby that if they sang, they would attract the whales. They leaned against the railing of the boat and in their loud, squeaky voices sang every children's song I had taught them. The adults surrounding them chuckled and smiled at them, but their mouths dropped open when the mother humpback and her calf sped toward our boat and swam under it, coming up on the opposite side, close enough to touch. To the delight of the boys, mother whale and baby performed for us for hours.

In northern Nova Scotia, a great horned owl alighted on the frame of our pop-up camper. Bears gorged on the blueberries growing in the thickets along the trail we hiked over, and much to the delight of the boys, Hurricane David blew in while we were huddled in tents at a primitive campsite deep in the woods, miles from anywhere. In Maine, we hiked around bogs and lakes in search of moose. Cubby, Mike, and Teddy froze with eyes as big as saucers when a huge bull passed two feet in front of them. Late at night we watched meteors streak across the star-speckled sky. After we had gone to bed in our camper, the little boys wiggled closer and closer to our bunk when the coyotes howled. Most nights, Charles and I would wake up to find Teddy and Cubby snuggled in with us. Mike would be sprawled out in a space for three, oblivious to the scary noises of the night.

Everything went exactly as planned that summer, but little did we know as we packed up our camping gear that we would never again enjoy such carefree innocence, that all our subsequent vacations would be taken in a frenzy to squeeze the most out of the little bit of time we had left as a complete and whole family.

CHAPTER 3

Treatment

TREATING HEMOPHILIA WITH HEALTHY BLOOD HAS BEEN A THEORETI-
cal possibility since the mid-nineteenth century. In 1840, a London
physician transfused blood from a healthy person into a hemorrhaging hemophiliac. The patient's bleeding stopped, and the physician realized that the donor's blood must contain something that is
not present in the blood of the hemophiliac–something that induces
clotting. This insight seemed of no practical use, however, since
transfusions would help one individual and quite mysteriously kill
the next.

It wasn't until the beginning of the twentieth century that Karl
Landsteiner, a pathologist in Vienna, recognized that the blood of
one person is not necessarily compatible with the blood of another.
Landsteiner noted that combining a drop of a subject's blood with a
drop of blood from someone else could cause the red cells to clump
together. Blood cells clumping together in a controlled sequence
and forming a patch at the site of a tear in a blood-vessel wall is essentially what clotting is all about. But the massive destruction of
red blood cells (hemolysis) caused by blood incompatibility, and the
resultant clumping of blood as it circulates through the body, result
in obstructions in the blood vessels, a collapse in circulation, and ultimately death.

Karl Landsteiner categorized human blood into four types, designated A, B, AB, and O. He received a Nobel Prize for this in 1930. An understanding of the ABO blood group and blood compatibility enabled physicians to perform transfusions with a higher rate of success, although patients who received transfusions of blood from an ABO-compatible donor still occasionally died. Rarely after a first transfusion but often immediately following a subsequent transfusion, a patient's blood cells would clump. This mysterious donor response to an apparently compatible transfusion prevented the use of whole blood as a routine treatment for hemophilia–or anything else, for that matter.

The risk of death by transfusion due to the massive destruction of red blood cells was not the only drawback to the use of whole-blood transfusions for the treatment of hemophilia. The amount of clotting factor that is contained in a unit of whole blood is small, and so the amount of whole blood required to stop a hemophiliac's hemorrhage would usually cause serious damage to the patient's internal organs. This in itself was life threatening.

Concurrently with the research on blood transfusions, other treatments for hemophilia were devised. In 1934, Dr. Hamilton Hartridge, a physiologist at the University of Oxford, discovered that certain snake venoms cause blood to clot. After testing many snakes, Dr. Hartridge and a colleague, Dr. Robert Gwyn MacFarlane, a hematologist, learned that the venom of the Russell's viper was the most effective. MacFarlane and Hartridge used this snake's venom to make a weak solution that was used to pack a bleeding socket in the mouth of a hemophiliac whose tooth had been extracted. The venom solution was effective, but though it could be used to treat bleeding in the mouth and external bleeding, it was far too toxic to be used systemically.

In 1937, the first blood bank in the United States opened at the Cook County Hospital in Chicago. Shortly afterward, in 1940, Karl Landsteiner, the pathologist who solved the mystery of ABO blood grouping, discovered that a protein similar to one found in the red blood cells of rhesus monkeys was present in human blood. More than 80 percent of humans are Rh-positive. That is, their red blood cells are coated with this protein. When coated cells come in contact with blood cells lacking the Rh factor, the noncoated cells form an antibody that surrounds the foreign invader, the Rh-positive cells. They are then destroyed, which leads to clumping within the blood vessels, causing, among other problems, the collapse of the circulatory system and the consequent death of the patient. Rh-negative patients tolerate a first blood transfusion because the antibodies that destroy the Rh-positive cells haven't yet developed fully. But such patients rarely tolerate a second transfusion because the antibodies are now ready to go into attack mode, and the assault on the Rh-positive cells is successful. The discovery of the Rh factor lowered the risk of blood transfusions significantly and was especially important to those patients, such as hemophiliacs, who require frequent multiple transfusions.

Cellular blood and plasma were successfully separated at the dawn of the twentieth century. During World War I, plasma was found to be an effective treatment for shock. Freeze-dried powdered plasma was reconstituted by the addition of sterile water, however, and the necessary equipment for the process was bulky and took precious time on the battlefield. Shortly before the United States entered World War II, Dr. Edwin Cohn, a Harvard biochemist, took up the challenge of separating plasma into fractions. His research resulted in the production of human albumin, a plasma protein that was a more effective treatment for shock on the battlefield, since a smaller quantity of albumin than plasma was needed. Albumin saved thousands of lives in World War II.

Albumin was useless to hemophiliacs because it does not contain clotting factor, but plasma was a vast improvement over whole blood because it caused fewer transfusion reactions and did not overload the liver with iron. The major disadvantage of plasma was that, like whole blood, it contains only minute amounts of clotting factor per pint. It was necessary to use large amounts to stop a bleed. This caused tremendous stress on the patient's circulatory system and was often deadly. When a hemophiliac was losing blood, it was sometimes impossible to pour enough plasma into his veins to raise the clotting-factor level high enough to stop the hemorrhaging. Despite all the medical progress made in the first six decades of the twentieth century, an ideal treatment for life-threatening hemorrhages in hemophiliacs did not exist until the mid- to late 1960s. Hemophiliacs were still unable to lead normal lives and could not anticipate a normal life span.

In 1964, while watching a bag of plasma thaw, Dr. Judith Graham Pool, a Stanford University researcher, noticed that stringy flakes appeared to be dropping to the bottom of the bag and settling there. Her tests of this precipitated material showed that it was composed of several of the clotting factors and that relatively large amounts of factor VIII had separated from the frozen plasma. Dr. Pool's subsequent development of a method to separate the clotting factors from the remaining plasma was a major breakthrough in the treatment of hemophilia.

Cryoprecipitate (referred to as cryo) was the name given to the product made from the clotting factors that Dr. Pool separated from the frozen plasma. It means, literally, a frozen substance that has separated out of solution. Cryoprecipitate made higher doses of clotting factor available to hemophiliacs without overloading their circulatory systems. It was a nearly but not quite ideal treatment for hemophilia. Like whole-blood and plasma transfusions before it, cryo usually required a trip to a hospital emergency room for treatment—and emergency room experiences have traditionally been frustrating and sometimes counterproductive for hemophilic patients and their parents.

Upon arrival at an emergency room, a hemophiliac was faced with the problem of convincing the staff that a hemorrhaging hemophiliac is a high-priority case even though to a harried triage nurse confronted with feverish babies and gaping wounds, a hemophiliac with a swollen joint is unimpressive. Indeed, a bump on the head with no neurological signs of damage *is* unimpressive looking, but if the emergency room staff waits long enough, the neurological signs of an intracranial hemorrhage will *become* impressive.

It is not surprising that the emergency room experiences of hemophiliacs have been less than ideal. The standard four-year medical curriculum devotes sometimes as little as two hours to instruction in coagulopathy.

"Hi there, Mrs. DePrince." It's Erik's school nurse. "Don't get alarmed— it's not critical. It's just that Erik has an ankle bleed. He can't walk, so I'll wheel him to the side door. Then he won't have far to go on crutches."

I pick up Erik at the middle school. He tries to convince me that his ankle is broken. I know it's not. Erik has always had difficulty admitting that he has a bleed. When he was younger, he would tell his friends that he had a football injury. I suppose to a child with a bleeding disorder, "football injury" sounds exciting.

Fortunately for Erik, this ankle-joint bleed isn't as bad as his last one. If we get it treated soon enough, there shouldn't be much permanent damage.

We arrive at the hospital. It's jam-packed with emergency room patients. Erik moans when he sees the crowd. "Oh no, it's going to be one of these visits."

I sign Erik in and tell the ER admissions clerk that he is a hemophiliac—no sense trying to explain a von Willebrand patient with a joint bleed; the textbooks claim there is no such animal. I explain to the clerk that Erik must have cryoprecipitate as soon as possible. She asks whether I think the ankle is broken. I admit that it isn't, so she tells me to sit down and wait our turn.

I notice a huge sign that says TREAT HEMOPHILIACS FIRST. Aha! I approach the triage nurse. She understands the problem. She checks Erik's ankle, and soon he is moved to a treatment area and told to sit on an examining table.

Erik sits on the table, which is good, because then he can elevate his leg. The bleeding will be worse if his ankle dangles. A nurse breezes by. I ask her for an ice pack, since Erik's ice pack from school has melted. "I can't give you an ice pack," she says. "You'll have to wait for the doctor to order it."

A doctor comes in and examines Erik's ankle. I remind him that information regarding my children is on file at the emergency room desk. He does recognize us, because this is the same physician who diagnosed Erik's pancreas hemorrhage as gas. Both he and his hospital know better now.

The physician suggests that "maybe we should X-ray the ankle before we order cryoprecipitate for Erik. If the ankle is fractured and it isn't a bleed he won't need the cryo." I roll my eyes. Erik rolls his eyes. We just look at the physician. "OK, OK," he says, "we'll type and cross match, then send him for an X ray while the blood bank is preparing the cryo."

The physician leaves, and Erik says, "He's learning, but if they keep X-raying me every time I have a joint bleed, I'll eventually glow."

Someone comes in to draw blood for typing and cross matching. Someone else arrives to wheel Erik down to radiology for the X ray of his ankle. The wheelchair has a broken leg extender. It happens to be the right leg extender. Erik's bleed is in the right ankle. His foot and ankle hang over the edge of the leg extender. He is in pain. The swelling has worsened significantly since we arrived in the emergency room over an hour ago.

When we return to the treatment room, another patient is on the table. She is lying still and wearing a neck brace. The nurse explains that there have been a few accidents, and space is tight. There are no more vacant examining tables. Erik is left sitting in the wheelchair. His ankle is still dangling. His pain is worse, and the foot is extended, meaning that there is now a lot of blood in the ankle joint.

We have already waited two hours for the cryo to arrive when I ask the nurse why it is taking so long. She answers, "It takes a very long time to thaw and pool that stuff." I know this is not true, but it's not worth an argument.

The woman on the table with the neck brace asks us what happened to Erik. We explain the situation to her. I ask her what happened to her. She answers, "Well, I was in an accident. I'm not really hurt, but I thought that I had better let them take me to the hospital in case I want to sue later. You never know." I feel like screaming.

The cryo arrives. Erik is hooked up, and it begins to drip. By the time the cryo is done dripping, we have been in the hospital emergency room for six hours. I know that Erik's ankle will be permanently damaged, and I am more determined than ever to use cryo at home.

Some patients are fortunate enough to be treated by hematologists who allow them to store, pool, and use cryo at home. This is far more efficient than using a hospital emergency room, but it is the exception rather than the rule. And even in the case of the rare patient who uses cryo in the home, the treatment isn't always convenient. Because of cryo's storage requirements, it cannot be carried around on vacation in a cooler chest nor stored in a college dorm refrigerator. Cryo works well in most cases but has definite limitations.

Clotting-factor concentrates that were more convenient and less complicated to use than cryoprecipitate were also developed in the mid-1960s and were greeted with much enthusiasm by hemophiliacs. In May 1966, the Food and Drug Administration licensed a factor VIII concentrate to Baxter of North America. In December 1968, the first factor IX concentrate was licensed, to Cutter (later a division of Bayer). Within the next decade, concentrates were licensed to other companies as well. There were no clotting-factor concentrates available in the United States for patients with von Willebrand disease until the late 1980s. Thus when the boys were growing up, those of us with von Willebrand disease—Adam, Erik, and I—used cryoprecipitate while Mike, Teddy, and Cubby—who had hemophilia A—used factor VIII concentrate.

The marketing of clotting-factor concentrates in the late 1960s and in the 1970s not only ushered in the golden age of hemophilia but also established four corporations–Alpha, Armour, Baxter, and Bayer–as the giants in the U.S. clotting-factor industry. The new clotting-factor concentrates offered tremendous advantages over cryoprecipitate. For the first time, clotting factor could be stored in a refrigerator, in a cooler chest, or at ambient temperatures. Factor concentrates were lyophilized (freeze-dried)–like instant coffee– and stored in little bottles under sterile procedures. In order to use the concentrate, it was necessary only to reconstitute it with a small amount of sterile water. Hemophiliacs were no longer homebound. Large chunks of their time need no longer be spent in hospitals. Concentrates offered better and more effective control of hemor- rhages. Hemophilia treatment centers were able to develop a home- care protocol for many of their patients, which meant less time spent in medical facilities, fewer days lost from work or school, and a reduction in the frequency of serious orthopedic problems. For the first time ever, hemophiliacs gained control over their bodies, and their lives.

The trails in the White Mountains of New Hampshire are rugged, and Charles and I decide to divide the family into two teams according to our various abilities to cope with the terrain. The DePrince family A team will consist of the strong hikers: Charles, Adam, Erik, and Teddy. Their goal is to reach the summit of the mountain. The De- Prince family B team will consist of the weaker, pokier hikers: Mike, Cubby, and me. Our goal is simply to get to wherever it is we manage to get when we meet the A team coming down.

The A team heads off at a brisk pace. The B team sort of meanders up the trail. We examine the wildflowers, admire a striped caterpillar, and look for signs of wildlife. Since Cubby is a member of the B team, there is a steady spate of chatter the whole way up and the whole way down. The A team occasionally encounters a bear on the trail. The B team seldom encounters anything larger than a chipmunk.

The B team is having a particularly pleasant day. We sit by a lake and watch a kingfisher dipping for its meal while we munch on our snacks. We stop by a minibrook that's gurgling down the mountain. We take off our hiking boots and sit on a rock, refreshing our tired feet in the cold, clear water. Finally we spy the descending A team. Its members look a bit worse for wear. "That trail was too difficult as it got to the top," complains Charles. "The trail guide didn't rate it correctly. There were these little cliffs. I had to pass Teddy up to Adam and Erik. Teddy and Adam each fell, but not on the cliffs. They tripped on rocks."

Teddy looks fine. "I tripped and bumped my head. I had to treat on the mountain," he explains as he holds his bruised forehead an inch from my eyes.

Adam has a blood-filled boot and a soggy sock. "My knee won't stop bleeding. It's been bleeding since the summit." The gash on his knee is deep. I try to apply pressure and tie a bandanna around it.

As we descend the mountain, the bandanna becomes blood soaked. Adam complains the whole way down about how unfair it is that he won't be able to hike the rest of the week because the knee probably won't stop bleeding. Little Cubby offers him the use of his factor concentrate. Adam explains that he can't use it. "It doesn't have what I need in it."

"Boy, you have rotten luck," Teddy tells him. "It's a shame you can't use factor."

"Just be thankful it's not your head, Adam," a very serious Cubby comments. "Then your brains would leak out, and the doctor wouldn't be able to put them back in because they'd get dirty when they fell on the trail. Mommy, can doctors wash Adam's brains if he gets cut and they fall out? Do doctors use dish detergent or laundry detergent? I bet they use shampoo. That's for the head. Mommy, are brains soft like pudding or hard like bagels? Mommy, if brains do fall out—"

A very bloody Adam begs, "Mom, please. My lifeblood is filling my boot, and he just rambles on and on. It's not like he's making any sense or anything."

But nothing deters Cubby. He's too curious. He just keeps asking question after question.

As I recall that day, I remember how easy and carefree life once was for my three sons with hemophilia A, and how much more vulnerable the three of us in the family with von Willebrand disease often felt, far from home and our freezer full of cryo.

CHAPTER 4

───✲───

Trade-off

FOR THE HEMOPHILIA POPULATION, TREATMENT HAD ITS PRICE. TREAT-
ment brought with it trouble in the guise of something so small that
only the most powerful electron microscope could view it, something so breathtakingly beautiful that one could stare for hours and
still be awed by its incredibly complicated structure. Something terribly dangerous.

Virus means "poison" in Latin. A virus is an incomplete organism
that manipulates the genetic material of a host's cells in order to re-
produce, mutate, and continue on its endless journey through the
ages. Many viruses are blood borne. The hepatitis B virus (HBV) is
a blood-borne virus that caused an epidemic among American
troops in 1942. At the time, HBV hadn't yet been identified, so the
disease was classified under the blanket term *homologous serum
hepatitis.* Ironically, this hepatitis epidemic resulted from efforts to
avoid an epidemic of a different virus.

In the late 1930s, Japan was aggressively attempting to dominate
eastern Asia, and in this country there was concern about the potential loss of troops to yellow fever if the United States entered a
war fought in tropical areas. Yellow fever is caused by a virus carried by mosquitoes and is a plague to wartime armies. Troops often
live in crowded, squalid conditions, with not enough to eat. Their
immune systems, weakened by their living conditions and exhaus-

tion, provide the perfect reservoir for the yellow-fever virus. Napoleon lost twenty-five thousand troops to yellow fever in less than a month in Haiti in 1800. During the Civil War, both sides lost men to yellow fever, which in the eighteenth and nineteenth centuries was prevalent in the Mississippi Delta, where it was ferried by boat to various ports along the river.

In 1939, in a plan to prevent yellow fever from endangering American troops, the surgeon general assigned to the Rockefeller Institute the responsibility of mass-producing millions of doses of a yellow fever vaccine. The project was a success, and the vaccine, prepared from human serum that was fractionated from the pooled plasma of thousands of donors, was available by the time the United States entered World War II in December 1941. The vaccine proved to be an effective deterrent to yellow fever, but there was an outbreak of another disease among the vaccinated troops. This disease caused fever, chills, anorexia, and fatigue. It turned the skin and eyes of the infected men a sickly shade of yellow.

Between 1942 and 1945, nearly a quarter of a million men who had been inoculated with the yellow fever vaccine developed hepatitis. Several hundred men died. Although the identity of the organism that caused this new epidemic was unknown, the vector was acknowledged to be the human blood serum used in the manufacture of the yellow fever vaccine.

At the same time that hepatitis was infecting yellow fever–vaccinated troops stationed in Africa and the South Pacific, other troops were developing hepatitis for a different reason. The blood products provided for battlefield casualties were powdered plasma and human albumin. These products, like the serum used for the yellow fever vaccine, were not derived from the blood of a single donor. The plasma was manufactured from the pooled plasma of 25 to 50 blood donors. The human albumin was manufactured from the pooled plasma of 250 to 2,000 blood donors. If one single donor in the pool had hepatitis, the entire lot of plasma was contaminated.

As a result of the World War II hepatitis epidemic, research on viral inactivation was conducted with the support of the Surgeon General's Commission on Measles and Mumps. The commission concluded that hepatitis present in human albumin could be inactivated if the albumin was diluted in a chemical solution and heated for ten hours at sixty degrees Celsius. It was decided that this form of viral inactivation would be practical in the large-scale preparation of human albumin solutions from large plasma donor pools, and the procedure was immediately adopted.

Of particular interest is the purpose of this study. Researchers wrote that the extensive administration of blood products in the preceeding years made the problem of hepatitis an important one and that epidemiological investigations strongly suggested that the risk of transmitting hepatitis was greater with the use of pooled plasma from multiple donors than it was from whole blood. The large size of the pools increased the probability that one or more donors would be infected with hepatitis, thus infecting the entire pool of plasma and consequently all recipients.

So half a century ago there was concern about the use of a plasma-fractionation product made from volunteer donors' pooled plasma. This concern was serious enough to prompt federally funded research aimed at solving the problem. Studies in the United States and Great Britain indicated a 4.5 to 7.3 percent hepatitis transmission rate in patients receiving volunteer donors' pooled plasma products, and this was years before prisoners, intravenous drug abusers, and people in undeveloped countries were paid to donate blood.

Since clotting-factor concentrate was first introduced in the mid-1960s, blood-borne hepatitis has haunted the hemophilia community. Some types of hepatitis were known, and some types were still unknown, when clotting factor was first licensed, but hemophiliacs were exposed to them all early and frequently. What made repeated viral infection from clotting-factor concentrates a near certainty were the plasma sources and the manufacturing process. According to records of the Centers for Disease Control, each lot of clotting factor was manufactured from the pooled plasma of up to twenty thousand donors. Currently, plasma pools of up to fifteen thousand donors are allowed if the plasma source is paid donors. Plasma pools of up to sixty thousand donors are allowed if the pool is composed of the plasma of volunteer donors. *The Journal of the American Blood Resources Association* reported that starting off with one large pool is less expensive than starting off with multiple small pools because the amount of labor is lower and the amount of purified product is higher.

There are simply not enough volunteer donors to fill the need for clotting-factor concentrate. The paid donors who are thus necessary can increase their plasma output through a process known as plasmapheresis. A liter of a donor's blood is siphoned off and separated into plasma and cells. The donor sells the plasma portion and the cellular portion is returned to him or her. Because the body replaces the plasma in a matter of hours, whereas it takes far longer to replace the cellular portion, a donor is able to donate plasma more frequently than he or she can donate whole blood. A whole-blood donor can donate blood only every eight weeks. A plasmapheresis donor can donate plasma as frequently as twice a week. One former donor reported that when he needed extra money, he would travel the circuit of plasma-collection centers, sometimes making four or five donations each week.

One can only wonder who would be desperate enough to donate their plasma twice a week for a payment of between five and forty-five dollars per unit. To find willing donors, companies that collected plasma often established their operations in poverty-stricken areas and in areas populated by intravenous drug abusers.

When clotting-factor concentrates flooded the market in the late 1960s and early 1970s, hepatitis was most prevalent in the intravenous drug abuser population, among homosexuals and prisoners, and in indigent populations. Nevertheless, a disproportionate amount of for-pay plasma was drawn from these groups. Some of the clotting-factor manufacturers lobbied for the passage of state laws that would enable them to buy plasma from prisoners. Arizona's state archives provide an example of this. Jack Pfister of the firm of Jennings, Strouss, Salmon, and Trask of Phoenix, Arizona, was assigned to represent Cutter just for this purpose. Pfister, who says that he was not told by Cutter that plasma collected from prisoners had a much higher rate of contamination with the hepatitis virus than that collected from the general population, testified on March 14, 1966, in favor of Arizona State Senate Bill 122, which provided for the sale of state prisoners' hobby items and blood.

A November 4, 1971, Department of Health, Education, and Welfare memo from Arlene Butterly, information officer for the Division of Biologics Standards, includes comments from prisoners at the Louisiana State Penitentiary at Angola. These prisoners explain that Hyland (Baxter) allowed them to donate plasma twice a week, whereas Cutter allowed them to donate it only once a week. It was the prison warden who finally limited their donations to once a week. This was in the interests of prison administration and had nothing to do with consideration for the safety of the blood supply.

The same memo acknowledges the government's lax control over imported plasma. Companies that made plasma products were inspected and licensed by the National Institutes of Health, but the collecting of plasma had never been subject to federal regulation. Though Butterly claimed that the NIH had plans to issue some regulations, the only federal requirement at that time was that companies that processed plasma had to file a report on where and how they bought it.

Butterly's memo mentioned that she learned from NIH records and other sources that human plasma was bought and sold on an international scale. She specifically mentioned that Armour used plasma from collection centers in Haiti and that Hyland (later a division of Baxter) used twenty-five hundred liters of plasma per month from a collection center in El Salvador.

In the early 1970s, Congressman Victor V. Veysey of California started to inquire into the safety of the nation's plasma supply. In an August 24, 1971, letter to Dr. Robert Q. Marston, director of the NIH, Congressman Veysey expressed concern that no steps were under way to end reliance on paid-donor blood despite the fact that the chances of contracting hepatitis were greater when a recipient received blood donated by paid donors than when he or she received blood donated by volunteers.

Dr. Marston's response to Congressman Veysey was that the level of hepatitis-associated antigen in commercial donors' blood was only six times as high as that of volunteer donors' blood. The actual incidence of clinical hepatitis was only three times as high. These figures were contradicted by numerous studies that indicated the risk to be from ten to seventy times higher. Marston's statistics, furthermore, were based on single-donor transfusions, not on the pooling of thousands of units of the plasma of high-risk donors. The use of pooled plasma in the production of products for the treatment of hemophilia resulted in a nearly 100 percent hepatitis-transmission risk rate for any hemophiliac who used clotting-factor concentrate before 1985.

"Mom, what's this all about? Look, there's this warning on the little kids' factor VIII boxes. It says that this product may carry a risk of hepatitis."

"Don't worry about it, Adam."

"But I am worried. How high is the risk? Could they get hepatitis? That's serious."

"I'm telling you not to worry about it, honey, because they've already had hepatitis."

"All three of them!"

"Yes, all three of them, and not just one kind of hepatitis, either."

"Oh wow! Why don't they just put a label on this that says GUARANTEED TO KILL YOU?"

"But then what would we do, Adam? Not use it?"

"Gosh, I don't know. Why don't they irradiate it or something? This is crazy. Do you think their livers are going to rot?"

On October 6, 1971, Congressman Veysey wrote another letter to Dr. Marston. He asked whether regulations existed regarding the importation of blood. Dr. Sam T. Gibson, then the acting director of the

Division of Biologics Standards at the NIH, responded to Congressman Veysey's letter. Regarding the shipment of blood, Gibson said, "At the moment no foreign establishments are licensed by this government to ship whole blood into this country." One should note the wording of this response. It does not say that whole blood was *not* being shipped into the country from foreign establishments, just that they were not licensed to do so. It also neglected to address the issue of blood plasma. This is a clear case of using semantics as an evasive maneuver. To the layperson, plasma is often called *blood,* but to the scientific community, *blood* refers only to whole blood.

Not one to be easily fooled, Congressman Veysey persisted in his efforts, and on November 3, 1971, he pressed the issue with Dr. Gibson: "You indicate no one is licensed to import whole blood into this country, but you omit reference to blood components."

Dr. Gibson finally replied, "Human plasma not intended for use as such, but destined for further manufacture by fractionation, or for the preparation of typing serum does come into this country from abroad under the short supply provisions of the Public Health Service Regulations, section 73:240." Though, according to Dr. Gibson, this plasma was not being used as plasma per se, it was being used for clotting-factor concentrates or other component products that were infused or injected into human beings.

The names and locations of some of the 1971 suppliers in the United States and abroad that fell under Public Health Service Regulation, section 73:240, reveal that the domestic suppliers were located in prisons and poor areas of large U.S. cities. Those from abroad were located in impoverished third world countries.

On January 28, 1972, *The New York Times* published an exposé of one supplier, Hemo Caribbean of Haiti, which was located in Port-au-Prince and owned by Joseph B. Gorinstein, an American stockbroker. The population of Haiti has the lowest per capita daily caloric intake of any group in the Caribbean. Tuberculosis, tetanus, gastrointestinal diseases, and malnutrition are rampant in Haiti.

The World Health Organization spoke out against the commercial use of plasmapheresis in developing countries with undernourished plasma donors. WHO was concerned that the sale of blood might become the principal source of income for people who were dependent on alcohol and drugs. And it questioned the danger for the recipients of some of the plasma derivatives, for example, hemophiliacs using clotting factors derived from donors at high risk for blood-borne diseases. The main reason for seeking out such donors was financial. A liter of plasma might be obtained for between two and four dollars in some developing countries, whereas it would cost from twenty dollars to forty dollars or more in some of the advanced countries.

Documents introduced as evidence in U.S. court cases and in a Canadian investigation confirm that during the late 1970s, Hyland imported three thousand liters of plasma per month from Lesotho, one of the poorest countries in Africa. Between 1985 and 1987, Armour received over a dozen shipments of plasma from Africa despite the fact that a 1985 WHO meeting in Bangui, the capital of the Central African Republic, had brought the African AIDS crisis to the attention of the world's scientific and medical community.

In 1972, Dr. J. Garrott Allen of the Stanford University Medical Center advocated labeling blood as having either a paid source or a volunteer source. Eventually, regulations were passed state by state requiring the labeling of bagged blood products, such as fresh-frozen plasma, packed red blood cells, and platelets. But labels were not required on clotting-factor concentrates and other manufactured blood components. Few if any hemophiliacs had any idea whatsoever of the source of the blood products they were being treated with.

Dr. Judith Graham Pool, the Stanford University researcher who developed a method of separating clotting factors from plasma in the mid-1960s, estimated in 1974 that if cryoprecipitate was used in their treatment, hemophiliacs in the United States would require factor VIII extracted from approximately 2.3 million pints of whole blood per year. If factor concentrate was used, they would require factor VIII extracted from approximately 6.5 million pints of blood. She pointed out that with nearly 8 million units of whole blood collected from volunteer donors per year, the raw material for safe and ethically acceptable factor VIII supplies was readily available if cryo was the treatment of choice. Pool expressed concern with the proposal for a new national blood policy that neither required nor encouraged the use of volunteer blood for this purpose. She described the purchases of plasma by pharmaceutical houses for use in the production of clotting-factor concentrate as "dangerous, expensive, wasteful, and unethical."

For many years, members of the hemophilia community were given no hints or clues that would have led them to believe that the product they were shooting into their veins was made from the plasma of tubercular Haitians or drug addicts with hepatitis. This wasn't indicated on the package insert. And the families of hemophiliacs around the country were being encouraged to sponsor blood drives. From the blood drives, they would earn credit toward the purchase of their clotting-factor concentrate.

Erik and Adam have helped me design a flyer using Mike's preschool picture. The flyer shows a grinning Mike. I check it over one more time. It reads:

> *This is our son, MICHAEL-NOAH DEPRINCE. He is three years old. He loves to play with Tonka trucks, Smurfs, and Matchbox cars. He likes to color, draw on walls, and dance. He enjoys splashing in puddles, digging in his sandbox, and swinging on his swing. He is affectionate, energetic and full of joy. He is also a hemophiliac, suffering with the most severe form of this disease. . . . We are asking you to help us provide a quality future for Michael-Noah by donating blood at the blood drive held in his name. . . .*
>
> > *BLOODMOBILE INFORMATION*
>
> *WHEN: Thursday, December 2, 1982, from 3:30 to 7:30.*
> *WHERE: At the BLOODMOBILE parked in front of the DePrince home.*
> *WHO: Anybody aged 17 to 66 who is in reasonably good health. Seventeen-year-olds must have signed permission from a parent or guardian. . . .*

THERE WILL BE AN OPEN HOUSE IN THE DEPRINCE HOME AT THE SITE OF
THE DRIVE DURING THE HOURS OF THE DRIVE. REFRESHMENTS WILL BE
SERVED.

Erik puts Mike and his Matchbox cars into our big red wagon.
Adam pulls him along while Erik and I put flyers into our neighbors'
mailboxes. The boys are excited about the event. They plan the kinds
of cake we'll serve to blood donors: chocolate chip, apple and pineap-
ple upside-down cakes.

During the following week, we receive dozens of responses to our
flyers. When the bloodmobile arrives, Charles runs the electric cable
to our outside outlet. The technicians who will screen the donors set
up at our kitchen table. Erik and Adam quiz them about their equipment. Erik is fascinated by the pot of colored fluid that is used to determine whether or not the donor is too anemic to donate. He wants
to see it work. I give permission for him to be tested. His little drop of
blood floats on top of the colored fluid. The technician laughingly
tells him that he is too anemic. Erik excitedly positions himself next
to this very pleasant technician. He wants to see the neighbors' drops
of blood sink into the fluid.

The dining room is set up as a refreshment buffet. The living room
is converted into a sign-up and waiting room. The family room becomes the playroom for the neighbors' children. The bloodmobile is
the actual blood-collection station.

The whole event takes on a carnival atmosphere as neighbors begin
to arrive. Over and over again, people tell me how happy they are to
be giving blood for Mike. Seven-thirty comes and goes. Donors are
still pouring in. Erik is still glued to the kitchen table. Adam is serving refreshments. Charles and I are mingling with all these generous
neighbors. Mike is running around, eating cake, and throwing
tantrums like any toddler who is overtired but won't admit it.

Mike gets too rambunctious. Charles carries his crying, protesting
son to bed. Nine o'clock has come and gone. Still there are donors
waiting in the living room. It's nearly eleven o'clock. The last donor
has left, and the bloodmobile is about to pull away. I feel good, really
good about this blood drive.

Like the neighbors who donated blood for Mike, the neighbors, friends, co-workers, and families of other hemophiliacs assumed that the blood collected in their antiseptic little neighborhoods was used to produce more clotting-factor concentrate. Unfortunately, this wasn't the way it worked at all. Hemophiliacs earned credit toward their clotting-factor costs for each donor who contributed to their drive. But the truth was that each time a hemophiliac infused himself with a dose of the early clotting-factor concentrates, he was receiving minute quantities of plasma from thousands of individuals from high-risk populations. More than a decade later, during a regional hearing of the Commission of Inquiry on the Blood System in Canada, a doctor said that he would rather eat a spoonful of someone else's sputum than infuse himself with the clotting-factor concentrate that was being produced in the 1980s.

The disease that would later become known as hepatitis B was the only serious recognized risk in the earliest factor concentrates, and hemophiliacs were so desperate that they were willing to tolerate the suffering that went along with the treatment. Hepatitis B symptoms build to a crescendo about two or more weeks after the onset of the disease, causing fatigue, anorexia, chills, fever, vomiting, diarrhea, and occasionally respiratory symptoms. Often these symptoms are accompanied by muscle and joint pain. Basically, HBV infection feels like a case of the flu. But with flu, the symptoms usually subside within three to five days. With HBV, they last two weeks.

The flulike symptoms are followed by what is known as the icteric phase, during which the liver, which gradually enlarged in the first stage, remains enlarged. The spleen and lymph nodes of the neck become enlarged. The bile duct may become obstructed, and the patient suffers upper abdominal pain. Jaundice, a yellowing of the skin, eyes, and mucous membranes, may occur because the damaged liver cells are unable to remove bilirubin (a product of red-blood-cell breakdown) from the blood.

Nausea, diarrhea, and vomiting generally worsen when the icteric phase begins. Then they gradually diminish. The yellowed skin is usually maddeningly itchy. Hives can develop. In a minority of patients, the kidneys can be damaged, but approximately 90 to 95 percent of individuals who contract HBV appear to recover completely in approximately six weeks, although many of them must face further consequences of the infection twenty to forty years down the line. For 5 to 10 percent of HBV patients, the disease takes a more serious course. Some of them die outright from severe liver damage.

For many hemophiliacs, hepatitis was a fact of life, even before the use of clotting-factor concentrates. Dr. Edward Shanbrom was the medical director of Hyland when Hyland's first two clotting-factor concentrates were developed. These products, Anti-Hemophilic Factor (AHF), licensed by the Food and Drug Administration in May 1966, and Hemofil, licensed by the FDA in January 1968, were factor VIII concentrates. They were both used to treat hemophilia A. When asked why Hyland produced a product pooled from the plasma of thousands of donors at high risk for hepatitis, Dr. Shanbrom later explained, "The thinking at the time was that anyone who received six or seven units of blood would have developed hepatitis. Hemophiliacs were always exposed to hepatitis. We thought that there was only one hepatitis at that time, hepatitis B. Since no test existed for hepatitis, we thought that hemophiliacs were already immune. That seemed to be a truism at the time because hepatitis wasn't really a problem with hemophiliacs then."

––––––––––

July 1986–A postcard of the Great Salt Lake arrives from my friend Mary and her family. She and her husband are on their dream vacation in the West. I turn the postcard over and read:

> *We spent a week in Utah. John felt car-sick one morning. I turned around to look at him and he was as yellow as a lemon. Luckily we were near a hemophilia center. They admitted him for non-A, non-B hepatitis. He's out today and feeling better, so off we go. You'd love it*

out here. It's all sky. We're having a great time. Heading up to Yellowstone now.

In May 1967, Dr. Saul Krugman, a professor of pediatrics at the New York University School of Medicine, published the results of studies he had been conducting for over a decade at New York's Willowbrook State School for retarded children. His research proved that there is more than one form of hepatitis.

Hepatitis A (HAV) is highly contagious. It is primarily transmitted among people living in crowded, unhygienic conditions. Hepatitis B (HBV), on the other hand, is less contagious by contact, but it is easily transmitted by injection or through transfusion.

Dr. Krugman's discovery of two different forms of hepatitis dovetailed with a discovery made in 1963 by Dr. Baruch Blumberg, a geneticist at the Institute for Cancer Research at Foxchase Center in Philadelphia and the Columbia University School of Medicine. Dr. Blumberg believed that people of different ethnic backgrounds, by virtue of their different genetics, respond to diseases differently. He collected hundreds of thousands of blood samples from many countries, and he and Dr. Harvey Alter, a hematologist with the NIH, discovered that antibodies in the blood of a New York hemophilia patient responded immunologically to something in the blood of an Australian aborigine. They called the discovery the Australian antigen, because they assumed that an antigen in the blood of the aborigine had provoked this response.

Dr. Blumberg tested the hemophiliac's antibodies with many other blood samples and discovered that they responded to the blood of leukemia patients also. This led him to conclude, wrongly, as it turned out, that the so-called Australian antigen was some sort of predictor for leukemia. In fact, the connection between the leukemia patients and the hemophilia patients was that they had all received transfusions.

Dr. Blumberg began to test the blood of hepatitis patients. He discovered that many of them tested positive for the so-called Australian antigen. Using Dr. Krugman's original blood specimens from hepatitis patients, Dr. Blumberg was able to determine that the Australian antigen was really the hepatitis B surface antigen (HBsAg), noninfectious particles of the hepatitis virus. The presence of these tiny particles in blood indicates that the donor of the blood has an active HBV infection. Dr. Blumberg's studies made it possible, therefore, to screen donor blood for hepatitis B. In 1971, the FDA licensed a test for HBsAg, and blood banks throughout the United States began testing blood for hepatitis.

Unfortunately, HBsAg does not appear in the blood until late in the incubation period of the disease. As a result, some patients with early hepatitis infections continued to donate infected blood. Considering that HBV infection has an incubation period of 45 to 180 days, it's easy enough to understand how the blood donation can be contaminated—especially if the blood is collected from a large group of high-risk donors. There is a good chance that one of them will donate blood during a window period of infectivity.

With the discovery of HBsAg, it became obvious that some patients with HBV infections have chronic active hepatitis: they never develop antibodies to the Hepatitis B virus, thus becoming lifelong carriers, capable of infecting others. Though most HBV carriers are asymptomatic, in some cases the chronic HBV carrier develops serious liver disease that produces cirrhosis.

Symptomatic or not, patients with chronic active HBV who frequently receive transfusions of blood products can become victims of hepatitis delta virus, also known as hepatitis D virus (HDV). The existence of this strange virus was totally unknown when the first factor VIII concentrates were marketed. The hepatitis delta virus can replicate only if it steals parts of the HBV to incorporate into its own structure. When the hepatitis delta virus infects a patient who has chronic active HBV, the resulting chronic hepatitis is usually more severe than that of HBV alone. The patient is at greater risk for rapidly developing cirrhosis. Death from liver failure occurs sooner. Cases in which a patient is infected with HBV and the hepatitis delta virus concurrently are referred to as HBV and HDV co-infection.

This condition is extremely severe and has a higher fatality rate than any other form of hepatitis alone or in combination.

None of this was known to the developers of early clotting-factor concentrate. But before they were to learn of the existence of HDV, there were more surprises in store for them.

In 1975, a blood test was developed for hepatitis A, and it became evident that still other hepatitis viruses existed. Posttransfusion patients had symptoms of hepatitis and yet were testing negative for hepatitis B and hepatitis A. For want of a better idea, or due to someone's lack of linguistic creativity, this other hepatitis virus was named non-A, non-B (NANB) hepatitis.

NANB hepatitis proved to be more than one virus. It is now known that hepatitis C (HCV) is the most common type of NANB hepatitis. It is responsible for approximately half the cases of NANB hepatitis. Fifty to 85 percent of hemophiliac patients who contract HCV develop chronic liver disease, yet widespread screening for evidence of HCV infection of donor blood wasn't instituted until 1989.

I'm waiting at the front door for Cubby's school bus. I have a few errands to run. Cubby will like that. For him, it means a trip to McDonald's. For me, it means good company.

"Mommy, Mommy, where are we going?"

After some teasing, I confirm that we are on our way to McDonald's.

"I don't want to go."

"WHAT!!! Why not?"

"I'm on a diet."

"Cubby, five-year-old kids do not go on diets."

"I hafta. I'm too fat. My tummy's too fat. The kids on the school bus call me Chubby Cubby."

"Oh, sweetie, that's not a fat tummy. It's your liver."

"Why's it so fat, Mommy?"

"It's not fat. It's just large. When you were real little, you caught this virus called hepatitis. It made your liver large. But I think that it makes you look cute, sort of like Santa's favorite elf."

"How did I catch the virus?"

"Somebody who was sick with the hepatitis virus donated blood. Their blood got used to make your factor VIII."

"What do I tell the kids when they say my tummy's fat? They're in kindergarten. They don't understand stuff like livers and viruses."

"Well, you understand it, Cubs."

"That's different."

"How about if you tell them this. Say, 'I don't have a fat tummy. That's my liver. It's large. Kids who have a large liver grow up to be tall and strong grown-ups. Kids who have a small liver grow up to be short and weak grown-ups."

"Wow! That's a great idea. But isn't that telling a lie?"

"Well, Cubs, it's not really telling a lie. It's sort of—well, sort of—"

"I know! I know! It's fiction!"

"Whoa, Cubs, good going, buddy. Where did you learn that big word?"

"Adam told it to me. He told me some of my books are fiction and some are nonsense."

———————

For some patients, liver damage escalates into the horrifying condition of hepatitis encephalopathy. Their blood-ammonia levels rise as a result of liver malfunction, and their brains are severely intoxicated by the ammonia. Tremors develop, followed by stupor, coma, and death. In some victims, the odor of the ammonia can actually be detected by a bystander. In one extraordinary case widely reported by the news media in the early 1990s, the odor from a woman with excessively high blood-ammonia levels was so strong that emergency room personnel fainted.

HBV has been demonstrated to be one of the causes of primary liver cancer in patients who contracted the disease early in life. Malignant liver tumors can develop twenty to forty years after an HBV infection. Similarly, HCV is implicated in the growth of malignant liver tumors years after the initial hepatitis infection. The incidence of primary cancer of the liver is thirty times higher in the hemophilia population than in the general population. The fact that it takes ten to twenty years or more for HBV and/or HCV patients to develop liver cancer is not comforting. Many hemophiliacs contracted these viruses during infancy. As they enter adolescence and young adulthood, they become cancer time bombs.

Cubby is unable to sit up or lie down. His liver and ascites (fluid in the abdomen) confine him to a reclining position. If he sits up, his enormously enlarged liver pushes his lungs and heart upward. If he lies down, his liver crushes his lungs.

The resident brings us Cubby's chest X ray. Cubby has been having more and more difficulty breathing lately. His immunologist in Newark wanted to see whether an X ray would show any signs of pneumonia.

As the resident hands me the large brown envelope with Cubby's X ray in it, he avoids my eyes. I ask, "What does the X ray show?"

The resident looks at the tops of his shoes. He answers, "Nothing. The X ray is fine."

As sick as Cubby is, he insists on seeing the X ray. I slide it out of the envelope and hand the huge film to Cubby. He has become much more medically sophisticated since that day six years ago when he asked about his big liver.

"Wow! Look at this X ray, Mom! There's hardly anything here. Just this big empty space, like a round window. That's the space my liver takes up. Wow! Look at my lungs. They're pushed way up! Mom, look. My lungs show above my collarbones.

"My heart is pushed to the right side of my chest and almost into my throat. This is a terrific X ray. I'll bet it's the most abnormal X ray that resident ever saw. That's why he looked at the floor instead of at me. Didn't he know that I can read X rays? Hey! Here comes Dr. Condoluci. Dr. Condoluci, come look at my X rays. Aren't they the most abnormal X rays you ever saw?"

Later in the day, Cubby proudly shows his X ray to his teacher, his brothers, and his dad. Cubby understands the implication of the X ray. He's an extraordinarily bright child. He and Mike are always into my medical texts.

Cubby knows he is dying, but like any little boy he's excited by weird and gross things. He derives great pleasure from this bizarre X ray.

It might be possible to forgive the manufacturers of clotting-factor concentrates for producing hepatitis-laden products in 1966, because they were unaware of the variety and complexity of the hepatitis viruses. At some point, however, the realization dawned that a problem existed, even though the precise scientific nature of the problem might not have been understood.

It appears logical that the wake-up call should have come in 1971 or shortly thereafter. After testing for HBV was instituted by blood banks, the rate of HBV among recipients of blood transfusions plummeted. The rate of HBV among the hemophiliacs using clotting-factor concentrate remained the same, however. After 1971, the presence of hepatitis B in clotting-factor concentrates should have been unacceptable.

Dr. Edward Shanbrom, who led the team of researchers at Hyland that developed the first FDA-approved clotting-factor concentrate, recalls that he knew there was a problem with the pooled plasma long before a blood test was devised to detect hepatitis A and decades before the development of a test for hepatitis C. Dr. Shanbrom learned of the problem by applying one of the most basic tenets of the scientific method—"observe." He noticed that the workers in the manufacturing plants where the factor VIII concentrate was processed began to come down with repeated bouts of hepatitis. This was occurring even though most of them weren't even making direct physical contact with the material being produced.

The infected employees worked close to the vats in which thousands of units of plasma were pooled and processed to produce factor VIII concentrate. Dr. Shanbrom concluded that the vats of pooled plasma were so infectious that the hepatitis was being transmitted by the vapors emanating from them. Since there were no tests for hepatitis at that time, Dr. Shanbrom studied the liver enzymes of the workers. Blood tests were done at regular intervals.

At first, Hyland was receptive to Dr. Shanbrom's concerns, but in the mid-1970s he was transferred to Baxter, the parent company, where he did clinical work for approximately two years while he was "debriefed," as he terms the process now. With the appointment of a new corporate president, Dr. Shanbrom's program of following hepatitis in the workers was discontinued.

After leaving Baxter, Dr. Shanbrom worked as a consultant, developing clotting-factor concentrates for other manufacturers. He recalls that during that time he also developed a detergent process for virally inactivating the concentrates. Though his process was experimental, laboratory evidence demonstrated that a detergent process would destroy not only enveloped viruses such as HBV and HCV but also thromboplastin, a fatlike substance in the plasma, and pyrogens, impurities that cause fevers in the hemophiliacs who received clotting factor. Because no one bothered to remove them, they were infused into the patient along with the clotting factor.

It is easy to understand how Dr. Shanbrom's detergent process worked if it is thought of as a dishwashing detergent. What makes a dishwashing detergent so effective is its ability to dissolve the grease on dishes. Certain viruses, including HBV, are enclosed in a lipid (fatlike) envelope. The detergent process simply dissolved the fatlike substances. With its lipid envelope destroyed, the virus was inactivated.

According to Dr. Shanbrom, he tried to persuade the four major manufacturers of clotting-factor concentrates to use a detergent process for viral inactivation as early as the mid- to late 1970s. Though some of the companies demonstrated interest in the process, there were no takers because, as Dr. Shanbrom recalls, "They said, 'We don't have a problem.' "

That they did have a problem should have been clear. The risk of transmitting hepatitis B to users of single-volunteer-donor blood products was low, whereas the risk to hemophiliacs using pooled paid-donor products was almost a sure thing.

Dr. Shanbrom says that he approached what was then the Hepatitis Division of the Centers for Disease Control, hoping to interest them in using and studying his detergent process of viral inactivation. The response was a letter from the CDC that he has saved to this day. The CDC expressed interest in Dr. Shanbrom's process but regretted that it did not have enough chimpanzees to enable researchers to conduct experiments with it. For want of adequate funding to the CDC for chimpanzees, clotting factor remained infectious.

Hemophiliacs were willing to exchange the risk of crippling and probable death from massive hemorrhage for the risk of possible death from liver disease. But they were unaware of the risk of almost certain hepatitis transmission. Warning labels on factor-concentrate packages understated the risks, and physicians minimized the seriousness of multiple hepatitis exposures. In retrospect, hemophiliacs are asking why their options should have been so limited for the two decades that passed between the licensing of the first clotting-factor concentrate and the licensing of the first dependable virally inactivated clotting-factor concentrate.

Dr. James Oleske, a specialist in pediatric infectious diseases who during the so-called golden age of hemophilia saw many pediatric hemophilia patients with hepatitis, became perplexed by the many infections he was seeing, and he believes that ethical questions should have been raised. "Patients shouldn't have had to accept that they were going to eventually get hepatitis." He believes that the leaders in the industry were distracted by "other issues."

On August 9, 1994, while being interviewed by Jane Wallace on her television program *Under Scrutiny*, Thomas Drees, the former chief executive officer of Alpha Therapeutics and now an activist for blood-safety issues, acknowledged that a virally inactivated product could have been developed. He further admitted that the problem was not so much an issue of cost as of inconvenience and lack of concern.

It is impossible to believe that in an era of unparalleled scientific progress a method of virally inactivating blood plasma could not have been implemented. Indeed, several patents were registered for viral inactivation of plasma products. Human albumin was successfully virally inactivated in 1945. Plasminogen was successfully virally inactivated in 1956. In both cases, the techniques involved heat treatment in solution at sixty degrees Celsius for ten hours. These patents make clear that the technology for treating clotting factors with heat was not out of reach; it just was not pursued avidly enough to make viral inactivation a reality for U.S. hemophiliacs before the mid-1980s.

In the late 1970s, a European company was perfecting a method of heat treatment of clotting factor. In 1978, Behringwerke Atkiengesellschaft (AG), a German company, developed a highly purified factor VIII concentrate heated in solution. It was called Humate-P (the P is for "pasteurized"), and it was marketed in 1980. Humate-P eliminated the possibility of passing hepatitis B to those who used it. In October 1981, Behringwerke offered its inactivation process to the U.S. plasma-fractionating industry. There were no takers. This decision was most unfortunate, because Behringwerke's pasteurization process was later proved to be effective against HIV as well as hepatitis B.

In March 1983, the FDA licensed what was intended to be America's first virally inactivated clotting factor, Hemofil T. Marketed by Baxter, this factor VIII product was made virally inactive through the use of a dry-heat treatment. By September 1985, all four of the major clotting-factor manufacturers were licensed to produce or market factor VIII products that had been virally inactivated by dry-heat treatment. By October 1984, two dry-heat-treated factor IX products had been licensed, and one factor IX product that was virally inactivated by a combination of chemical and dry-heat treatment.

Using dry heat to inactivate viruses in the clotting factors was not completely effective, although it was less expensive than the method of heating in solution and therefore more attractive to manufacturers. There is evidence that at least one of the four major manufacturers of clotting factor was aware that its dry-heat treatment did not eliminate HIV from its product. In 1985, Armour sent specimens of its dry-heat-treated factor VIII to two different U.S. laboratories in order to evaluate the efficacy of the treatment in eliminating HIV. Both laboratories detected the presence of HIV. There is no evidence that this was reported to the FDA at that time, and the contaminated product continued to be distributed in the United States. Eventually it was recalled. Armour then marketed the contaminated product in Canada.

By April 1986, a safer virally inactivated clotting-factor concentrate was finally licensed by the FDA. This was a Cutter product, Koate HS. One month later the FDA licensed Behringwerke's Humate-P, the proven, effective product, heat-treated in solution, that had been available to European hemophiliacs for more than half a decade. By the time U.S. manufacturers successfully virally inactivated clotting factor, some ten to twelve thousand hemophiliacs in this country had already been given a death sentence. Scientists who worked on the heat-treatment process admitted that once they were given the funds and the go-ahead, they discovered that viral inactivation was easier to achieve than they had previously believed. One scientist claims that before AIDS appeared on the scene, he had been alotted only one week in which to work on viral inactivation.

CHAPTER 5

Disaster

THOUGH BORN WITH HEMOPHILIA, ALL THREE OF MY ADOPTED SONS were otherwise healthy on July 6, 1982, when Dr. Louis M. Aledort, co-director of the National Hemophilia Foundation, received a grim letter from Dr. Bruce Lee Evatt of the Centers for Disease Control. Mike was three years old. Teddy was twenty-two months old, and Cubby was nearly eleven months old. Evatt wrote regarding the Kaposi's sarcoma opportunistic infection epidemic, which would, within days, be renamed the AIDS epidemic:

> As I mentioned over the phone, we have been quite concerned about the possibility that the causal agent is a virus. This agent appears to be producing immunosuppression as the underlying pathology. Because of the population of patients involved we have been suspicious that it may be transmitted in a manner similar to hepatitis, and thus creates a problem for users of blood products. Hemophiliacs would be prime candidates to develop this syndrome. We have had 3 reports of marked immunosuppression and opportunistic infections occurring in patients with hemophilia; one in Florida, one in Colorado, and one in Ohio. One of these patients was 62, one age 59, and the latest 27. These patients had no known cause for immunosuppression and were similar in presentation to the diseases seen in the Kaposi Sarcoma–Opportunistic Infection outbreak.

It is important that we are kept abreast of infections in hemophiliacs in order that recommendations on blood products can be made. We greatly appreciate your assistance in this manner as the hemophilia center would account for a large population of the hemophiliacs using concentrates.

None of the three hemophiliacs with AIDS mentioned by Dr. Evatt had been treated with the same lot of factor VIII concentrate. Considering the large number of single-dose vials of factor VIII that were produced in one lot (five hundred to twenty-five hundred), the implications of three separate lots being infected were horrific. Depending on the distribution of the vials from the infected lots of factor VIII used by each of these three patients, dozens, hundreds, or even thousands of hemophiliacs could have been infected at this point. It was feasible that just a handful of blood donors with AIDS would be capable of infecting the nation's entire supply of clotting-factor concentrate.

Three weeks after Dr. Evatt raised the alarm with Dr. Aledort, on July 27, 1982, the U.S. Public Health Service held the first of several meetings to address the issue of transfusion-acquired AIDS and the safety of the U.S. blood supply. Those who attended were representatives of powerful citizen-advocacy groups, government agencies, and the blood-banking industry: the National Gay Task Force, the National Hemophilia Foundation, the New York Group on Kaposi's Sarcoma and Opportunistic Infections, the Centers for Disease Control, the Food and Drug Administration, the National Institutes of Health, the New York City Health Department, the Office of the Assistant Secretary for Health, the American Association of Blood Banks, the American National Red Cross, the American Blood Resources Association, the Council of Community Blood Centers, and the Pharmaceutical Manufacturers Association. The actions that the group chose to take, or not take, after this meeting would have far-reaching consequences for blood-transfusion recipients.

The official Public Health Service report on the minutes of this meeting in July accurately records, according to people who were there, the statements that were made by representatives of the various factions.

There are 11,000 to 15,000 persons with hemophilia in the United States.... The Factor VIII normally present in fresh plasma is heat-labile and inactivated by many types of chemical or physical treatment. For this reason, the techniques developed for the production of Factor VIII concentrate from fresh plasma are known to have little effect on hepatitis viruses.... Lots of Factor VIII concentrate are prepared from plasma pooled from 1,000 to 5,000 donors. Donors come from many parts of society.

Almost all patients regularly receiving Factor VIII or cryoprecipitate develop hepatitis B and nonA-nonB infections. These products have been shown to transmit these infections. Because of the freedom and reduction of suffering permitted hemophilia patients by Factor VIII concentrate, the product's benefits are perceived by patients to vastly outweigh currently known risks.

There is urgent need to determine practical techniques to decrease or eliminate the infectious risks from Factor VIII. Several experimental means of accomplishing this are currently being evaluated.

There are factual errors in this report, not least of which is the statement that factor concentrate was "prepared from plasma pooled from 1,000 to 5,000 donors." A Department of Health, Education, and Welfare report published in 1976 documented the number of plasma donors per lot as being as high as twenty thousand. It is unlikely that the number of donors had decreased by the time of the meeting in 1982, since the CDC's *Morbidity and Mortality Weekly Report* documented the same size lots in 1983.

To allow factor VIII's heat lability and sensitivity to chemical and physical treatment to stand as an alibi for inadequate factor-production techniques in July 1982 was deceitful. Not only did industry representatives at this meeting know of the successful viral inactivation technique used by Behringwerke AG, but their companies had been offered the use of the process nine months before. In addition, *Arzneimittel-Forschung,* a German pharmaceutical journal, had published a paper written by Behringwerke scientists in 1981 entitled "Factor VIII Concentrate, Highly Purified and Heated in Solution."

American manufacturers now claim that in 1982, Behringwerke was able to produce only enough of their virally inactivated product (Humate-P) to treat one hundred hemophiliacs. They also claim that their "internal studies" showed a 90 percent loss of factor VIII potency in the manufacturing process, despite the fact that Behringwerke's loss was far less. During its investigation of HIV in the nation's blood supply in 1994, the Institute of Medicine was unable to obtain a clear idea of the reasons for these discrepancies. Members of the hemophilia community are extremely skeptical of the manufacturers' claims.

One of the three recommendations resulting from the July 1982 meeting was that the FDA's Blood Products Advisory Committee (BPAC) convene a panel that fall to discuss and evaluate practical techniques to decrease or eliminate the risk of infection from clotting-factor concentrate. The transcript of the later meeting clearly states that, "it has been more than two years since at least two different methods have been published, the Behringwerke method and the immune inactivation method." Some of the same people who attended the July 1982 Public Health Service meeting were present at the FDA's meeting in December of that year. One can only wonder how these people could have remained silent at the July meeting when it was recommended that "there is an urgent need to determine practical techniques to decrease or eliminate the infectious risks from Factor VIII. Several experimental means of accomplishing this are currently being evaluated."

Dr. Evatt, now chief of the Hematologic Diseases Branch of the CDC, believes that in July 1982 it might have been possible to have obtained emergency approval from the FDA for the Behringwerke product. The industry's failure to make this effort cost the lives of many hemophiliacs who were not yet infected that summer.

The July Public Health Service report referred to "donors from many parts of society" as the source of plasma for the manufacture of clotting-factor concentrate. "Donors from many parts of society" is a euphemism for the homeless, the poor, prisoners, migrant laborers, intravenous drug abusers, and impoverished citizens of developing nations, where diseases such as hepatitis and malaria are endemic. One unsettling comment made in the report is that "almost all patients regularly receiving Factor VIII or cryoprecipitate develop hepatitis B and nonA-nonB (NANB) infections." According to Dr. Oscar Ratnoff, then the director of the Hemophilia Treatment Center at the University Hospitals of Cleveland, cryoprecipitate did not carry the same high risk of viral transmission. This has been confirmed by retrospective studies. To equate the two treatment protocols was both misleading and disingenuous, but served the blood-banking and plasma-fractionating industries' wish to avoid a return to treatment with cryo.

Cryoprecipitate was produced almost exclusively on a large scale by the American Red Cross, a nonprofit corporation. Factor concentrate was produced by for-profit corporations. The Public Health Service reported in 1982 that hemophilia A patients used large amounts of factor VIII (forty thousand to more than sixty-five thousand factor units per year). Estimates of the size of the hemophilia A population in 1982 range as high as seventeen thousand. However, even if one uses the Public Health Service report's low estimate of eleven thousand to fifteen thousand, it is clear that approximately seven hundred million to one billion units of factor VIII were used by U.S. hemophiliacs. There were also two or three thousand hemophilia B patients and a small number of von Willebrand patients who used clotting factor. If these customers had given up their clotting-factor treatments and returned to cryo, approximately two hundred million to three hundred million dollars in annual retail sales of clotting factor would have been lost.

The Public Health Service's July 1982 report oversimplifies the feelings of the hemophilia population about contaminated clotting factor. Many hemophiliacs were unaware of their option of using the safer, volunteer-donor cryo. They were certainly unaware of the successful viral-inactivation process offered to the industry by

Behringwerke, just as they were unaware of Dr. Shanbrom's efforts to improve the processes by which clotting factor was produced. No information on these techniques had been disseminated to the consumers. Nor was this information present in the Public Health Service report, which presents viral inactivation as being in an experimental stage. Yet hemophiliacs in Germany, including at least one child of a U.S. military family stationed there, were using Behringwerke's Humate-P by the date of this meeting.

I am preparing dinner when the telephone rings. It is a Pennsylvania father of a hemophiliac. He has been given my name by Julie Frenkel, the Hemophilia Association of New Jersey's social worker. Because Cubby had already disclosed his HIV status to the press several months before (November 1990), the father was wondering whether I would be interested in participating in a class-action lawsuit against the manufacturers of Cubby's clotting-factor concentrate. The class action would be composed of children who were HIV infected.

I am aghast at the suggestion. I explain that I truly believe that these companies could not possibly have averted this disaster. "What options did any of us have?" I innocently ask him. "This was an act of fate. What could the manufacturers have done about it before it happened?" He has no concrete facts to give me, so I opt out—only to file three lawsuits against these companies in behalf of my children almost three years later. But by then, I know this was not an act of fate.

Despite the vociferous arguments of the Centers for Disease Control regarding the disaster about to befall the nation's blood supply, the conclusions and recommendations that came out of the July 1982 meeting were pitifully inadequate. The report concludes:

- The new "pathologic process" would be named acquired immunodeficiency syndrome (AIDS).
- AIDS has characteristics that suggest it is infectious.

• There is "an increased risk of AIDS for homosexual men, i.v. drug abusers, and among Haitians who have recently entered the United States." The pneumocystis pneumonia acquired by three hemophiliacs might also have been a consequence of AIDS; therefore, "high priority should be given to obtaining information that will answer this question."

• There is a need to determine whether the use of blood products is a risk factor in the transmission of AIDS.

The Public Health Service recommended:

• A surveillance system should be developed with the cooperation of the National Hemophilia Foundation and hemophilia treatment centers to determine whether any other hemophilia patients were demonstrating signs and symptoms of AIDS.

• Laboratory studies of hemophilia patients should be conducted to determine whether patients with hemophilia, especially those with suspicious disorders, were demonstrating signs of immune incompetence.

Hemophilia treatment centers throughout the United States immediately instituted the recommended surveillance of their patients. Six months later, Dr. Donald Francis, a virologist and researcher at the CDC, looked at the results of the study and commented, shockingly, that "for hemophiliacs I fear it might be too late. If the T-4/T-8 [white blood cell] prevalence data collected to date are reflective of pre-AIDS, ⅕ to ½ of hemophiliacs might already be exposed."

Before the identification of the virus responsible for AIDS, the most significant sign of the disease was the number of circulating T-lymphocytes, a special type of white blood cell that is important to the body's defense against disease. The average adult has a count of approximately seven hundred to thirteen hundred T-4-lymphocytes per cubic millimeter of blood. The normal ratio of T-4 lymphocytes to T-8 lymphocytes is two to one. Reversed ratios, such as Dr. Francis was seeing, signified the destruction of T-4 cells and were a predictor of AIDS.

From transcripts of the FDA's BPAC meeting in December 1982, one learns that not all members advocated viral inactivation of clotting-factor concentrates. Dr. Aledort of the National Hemophilia Foundation presumed to speak for all hemophiliacs when he asked, "What are the trade-offs, and what are we talking about in terms of yields? What will be the cost impact of this on the recipients in a very high reimbursement milieu, in which the banks are being broken already by treatment protocols?"

Later Dr. Aledort argued:

> I think that at the moment one has to recognize that high purity factor VIII has losses up to about ninety to ninety-five percent of the original source material. Intermediate purity product is about seventy-five to eighty percent. The cost is quite high now in the average hemophiliac. Cost from producer is approximately $5,000 to $6,000 a year without any add-ons from pharmacies, blood banks, et cetera. There are many families with more than two children with hemophilia.... So I think that we are already well beyond what is acceptable technologically, as far as I am concerned.... I don't see how we are going to get anywhere better unless you are really going to make a perfectly sterile product. I know that the market management is going to look to increasing the price by fifty percent, and there is an enormous potential of intimidation of the recipients that this is "sterile," and this is a better thing for you. I am not sure it is a better thing for them, and if I was more convinced it was, then I think one would begin again to negotiate and see. There are too many unknowns.

Dr. Aledort was correct about one thing here. There were families with more than two hemophilic children. Some of these families had only hemophilic children. If these families had been informed of the facts and available options and asked whether they would rather pay a higher price for their children's clotting factor or have them use the deadly lower-priced product, there probably would have been no question about the choice they would have made. The irony of Dr. Aledort's posturing regarding the higher cost of a virally inactivated product to his patients is the ultimate financial cost of

AIDS treatment. The cost of AIDS-related medical care for my own children has totaled nearly three million dollars. The emotional and physical toll has been inestimable.

Dr. Aledort's concern should have been not the piggy banks of his patients and their families but their health. The choice of product should have been given to the patients and their parents. As co-director of the National Hemophilia Foundation, Dr. Aledort should have insisted that the organization pass on to its members information regarding viral inactivation.

Since one manufacturer could not have been expected to provide the clotting factor for the entire world, one option Dr. Aledort could have suggested was that Behringwerke's product be made available to the U.S. hemophilia population for critical bleeds—life-threatening hemorrhages that would require expedient infusion without the fuss of typing and cross matching. Cryoprecipitate collected from volunteers in low-incidence areas could then have been used for non-critical bleeds while U.S. manufacturers adopted Behringwerke's technology. Treatment options could have existed.

Many volunteer plasma-collection centers existed in relatively low-risk areas. Female donors were also statistically a better risk than males. When the manufacturers needed clean plasma for studies, they knew where to get it. According to a July 18, 1996, *Philadelphia Inquirer* article by Donna Shaw, "Baxter separated out 'low bio-burden plasma'—which contained little or no hepatitis virus—to make the heat-treated Factor VIII that it then tested on chimpanzees."

At the December 1982 meeting of BPAC, a discussion ensued regarding the ability of the American Red Cross to produce enough cryoprecipitate to meet the needs of U.S. hemophiliacs. Dr. Lewellys Barker, vice president of blood services for the Red Cross, suggested that in light of the apparent link between hepatitis B and clotting-factor concentrates, those who treated hemophiliacs might consider temporarily returning to single-volunteer-donor cryo as the treatment of choice. His suggestion was not well received—not because of the inconvenience to the patient but because of the possible inconvenience to the Red Cross. If this was truly an operations problem for the Red Cross, it should have been jointly solved by the blood-banking industry and the appropriate government agencies rather than being dismissed outright. But one cannot ignore the possibility that the switch to cryo posed too great a threat to the bottom line of for-profit manufacturers.

Dr. Aledort's statements to the effect that 75 to 95 percent of the product was lost during the viral-inactivation process was challenged at the BPAC meeting by Dr. Robert J. Gerety, director of the Hepatitis Branch of the Division of Blood and Blood Products at the FDA's National Center for Drugs and Biologics. As recorded in the transcripts, Dr. Gerety was so surprised by Dr. Aledort's statement that he needed to clarify what he was hearing:

> I would just like to . . . see if I really heard what I thought I heard. You would rather leave the viruses in the product that is administered by parents, that is shipped in interstate commerce, and that goes into newly diagnosed hemophiliacs and the ten percent of sero-negatives rather than attempt to remove [them]? . . . You would rather leave it the way it is, knowing that there are viruses in there . . . than to attempt to remove the viruses that we know we can remove with a procedure . . . that retains eighty-two percent of activity in the experimental setting–and I have all the faith in the world that the industry can do a better job.

Dr. Margaret Hilgartner, medical director of the Regional Comprehensive Hemophilia Treatment Center of New York Hospital–Cornell Medical Center, backed Dr. Aledort's position. "The hepatitis can be handled," she said. "I think the liver biopsies study has shown that the pathologic problems in the liver are not that severe, and we don't have people dying of overwhelming hepatitis and we don't have people dying of cirrhosis. So at the moment it can be handled. We have a hepatitis-B virus vaccine for our newborns."

How well hepatitis was being handled is questionable. Liver disease was then the number-two cause of death among hemophiliacs. As for newborns, many children born with hemophilia have no family history of the disease. In such cases, the first indication that a child has hemophilia is the initial hemorrhage. In 1982, this meant treating the newborn with a virally contaminated product before a vaccine was ever given. And although hemophilic children with a family history of the disease sometimes had the opportunity to receive the hepatitis B vaccine before a first hemorrhage necessitated treatment with clotting-factor concentrate, that did not necessarily mean they were protected. This is because the HBV vaccine regimen includes three doses: the second dose is given one month after the first, and the third is given five months after the second. In approximately 70 percent of patients, an antibody response to the vaccine isn't detectable after the first dose, and 10 percent of patients never develop antibodies in response to the vaccine.

If a newborn with hemophilia was fortunate enough to be diagnosed before the first hemorrhage and fortunate enough to be one of the 30 percent to produce antibodies to HBV after the first dose of vaccine, then he had little to fear from HBV. If he wasn't as fortunate— well, then he contracted HBV despite the existence of the vaccine.

It was generally acknowledged at the December 1982 BPAC meeting that there was a high rate of hepatitis B infection among hemophiliacs. "I think the Panel in closed session has to recognize that in the hemophiliac population that we are talking about, ninety percent currently have B marker," Dr. Aledort said. "So we are talking about ten percent of the population with no markers, who gets repeatedly exposed to this material, and we don't even know why those ten percent don't have markers. We are talking about a very small percent who may never convert, who probably have had exposure to B. That has to be understood as part of the trade-off."

Interpreting from the transcript, it appears that Dr. Aledort's hypothesis was that 90 percent of hemophiliacs were already infected with HBV, so why bother to virally inactivate the products they were being treated with? Dr. Aledort did not address the issue of the remaining 10 percent of twenty thousand hemophiliacs. Nor did he respond to a question from Dr. Joseph Bove, chairman of the Committee on Transfusion Transmitted Diseases of the American Association of Blood Banks, about the 100 percent of new patients (newborns and young children) who had not been exposed to HBV.

Early in 1983, Dr. Donald Francis of the CDC wrote to a colleague, Dr. Jeffrey Koplan, about a meeting that had been held on January 4 of that year by the Public Health Service's Workgroup to Identify Opportunities for Prevention of Acquired Immune Deficiency Syndrome. He was not encouraging about the future:

> The members failed to agree on recommendations for the best means at this time for decreasing the chance of blood/blood-product-associated AIDS. I feel there is a strong possibility that some post-transfusion AIDS and much post-factor-VIII-receipt AIDS will occur in this country in the coming two years. As it is ïCDC's responsibility to take every opportunity to eliminate AIDS transmission, I think CDC should come out with its own recommendations.

Dr. Francis made seven recommendations to Dr. Koplan. Five of them concerned stringent blood-donor-deferral guidelines. There was still no test to identify AIDS in potential blood donors, but since most AIDS patients also tested positive for hepatitis B, Dr. Francis suggested that the hepatitis B core antibody test, a far more sensitive test than the HBsAg test then used to screen blood, was a good temporary substitute. This recommendation could very well have prevented the transmission of AIDS to 90 percent of the approximately twelve thousand nonhemophilic transfusion recipients who were infected during the following two years.

Dr. Francis's final recommendation, involving factor VIII use, was that

> only small pool (less than 100 donors) concentrate or cryoprecipitate be used on hemophiliacs starting immediately (after supplies become available). This recommendation should stand until either: 1) knowledge of AIDS permits more accurate recommendations or 2) plasma becomes available which has been collected using the previously stated donor deferral.

Dr. Francis's memorandum to Dr. Koplan seems to indicate that it was possible for the CDC to make strict recommendations for the collection of blood:

> I understand that these recommendations will be controversial and that there will be objections by industry and blood bankers. I think we should get comments from these groups and should keep them informed of our to-be-published recommendations. However, to wait for their approval of our recommendations will only endanger the public's health.

The strong measures urged by Dr. Francis were based on his frustration with the January 4, 1983, meeting of the Public Health Service work group. The purpose of that meeting was to develop recommendations that would decrease the incidence of transfusion- and infusion-related AIDS. Unfortunately, philosophical disagreements on the ethics and political correctness of donor deferral and disagreements about surrogate testing (hepatitis core antibody testing) of donors dominated the conference. Thus, nothing worthwhile was accomplished.

The frustration expressed by Dr. Francis was echoed by John Hink, an industry representative, in a report to Cutter on January 6, 1983: "Difficulties in communication and political power struggles made progress toward these objectives difficult. The anti-discrimination position of the gays, self-serving comments of blood bankers, and lack of data to provide legitimacy to many proposals resulted in an overall stalemate."

According to Hink's notes on the January 4 work-group meeting, Dr. Aledort commented, "How do we know we accomplish anything by running tests and excluding donors; if everybody runs tests, where are our controls?"

If asked, the hemophilia community would have refused to sacrifice its members' lives for the scientific method. There would be nothing valuable enough to learn through experiments in which "risk versus benefit" was so high.

On January 6, 1983, the day John Hink wrote his report to Cutter, the Committee on Transfusion Transmitted Diseases of the American Association of Blood Banks held a meeting. Participants included representatives from the American Red Cross, the Council of Community Blood Centers, the American Blood Commission, the CDC, the FDA, the National Hemophilia Foundation, the National Gay Task Force, and the American Blood Resources Association. This meeting, like all others of that era, was top-heavy with representatives of trade organizations for the manufacturers of blood-component products but light on representatives of blood-product consumers.

A Joint Statement on Acquired Immune Deficiency Syndrome Related to Transfusion was issued. Though several sensible, appropriate, and long-overdue recommendations emerged, one recommendation was totally out of sync with the clear and present danger. The meeting's participants agreed to recommend that because the transmission of AIDS via blood and blood products other than clotting-factor concentrate had not been proved, it would not be prudent to violate the civil rights of any group of citizens by excluding them as donors. This reflected a concern for political correctness that went far beyond the limits of safety. It was also recommended that blood banks need not institute surrogate testing, that is, testing for hepatitis B core antibody to indicate whether a potential donor might have AIDS.

By January 6, 1983, more than eight hundred cases of AIDS had been reported. The large majority of them were in the gay community. Intravenous drug users and recent Haitian émigrés also had a high rate of AIDS. Eight hemophiliacs had been diagnosed with AIDS, and two more cases were highly suspect. None of these eight members of the hemophilia population had any other high-risk characteristics. One of them was a ten-year-old child. Yet this meeting of the American Association of Blood Banks concluded that "the cause of AIDS is unknown ... evidence for its transmission by blood is inconclusive."

A twenty-month-old baby boy in San Francisco had been diagnosed with AIDS in September 1981—nearly one and a half years before this meeting of the AABB. The baby had received numerous blood transfusions shortly after birth. One of his donors, a middle-aged man, had subsequently been diagnosed with AIDS. This case of AIDS transmission could not be explained away. The infant was not Haitian. He was not a hemophiliac. He was not gay.

The recommendations of the AABB in January 1983 did nothing to halt the progress of the AIDS epidemic within the hemophilia community. The recommendations did nothing to prevent AIDS from spreading to the nonhemophilia population of blood-transfusion recipients.

Throughout the early days of the transfusion-transmitted AIDS epidemic, the National Hemophilia Foundation did not act in the best interest of its constituency. Dr. Evatt had not minced words in his July 6, 1982, letter to Dr. Aledort: "Hemophiliacs would be prime candidates to develop this syndrome." This sentence cannot be construed as anything other than a warning.

In response to Dr. Evatt's letter, the National Hemophilia Foundation issued its first "Hemophilia Patient Alert" on July 14, 1982. The NHF informed its constituency of the three hemophiliacs then known to exhibit symptoms of what would soon be called AIDS but advised, "It is important to note that at this time the *risk* of contracting this immunosuppressive agent is *minimal* and CDC is not recommending any change in blood-product use." This advice was emphasized in large uppercase letters at the bottom of the page:

IMPORTANT
REMEMBER, CDC IS NOT ADVISING A CHANGE IN TREATMENT REGIMEN AT THIS TIME. IF THERE ARE ANY QUESTIONS, CONTACT YOUR PHYSICIAN OR HEMOPHILIA TREATMENT CENTER.

In 1995, Donald Francis was the first witness to be called before the Commission of Inquiry on the Blood System in Canada. During his testimony, Dr. Francis acknowledged that he and Dr. Evatt were the NHF's primary contacts at the CDC. Dr. Francis testified that neither he nor Dr. Evatt ever recommended that there not be a change in treatment regimen of hemophiliacs. He testified that he couldn't even remember being asked. Dr. Francis said, "I remember very clearly conversations that Bruce Evatt and I had, both [of us] saying that if our children were hemophiliacs we would take them off factor VIII immediately." In a deposition taken at the Justice Department in 1995, Dr. Evatt confirmed this conversation. He also testified that he had warned in an article written for the December 3, 1982, issue of the CDC's *Morbidity and Mortality Weekly Report* that hemophiliacs "should be advised" of the possible risks associated with the use of clotting-factor concentrate. A draft of his article, including the warning, was sent to the clotting-factor manufacturers. A week later, when the article was published, Evatt's warning had been deleted. He has "no idea" why the warning was omitted and by whom—government or industry?

It's too hot to cook today. Charles and I decide to take the boys out for dinner. Mike is only three. He's at that picky age when he'll eat only one thing for weeks at a time. This time it's pancakes. Erik and Adam, at eight and nine years old, will eat anything. For Mike's sake and my sanity, we decide to eat at the International House of Pancakes.

We run into another hemophilia family. They've decided to eat out also. We've hardly greeted each other when Bea, the mom, shielding her face with her hand, whispers something inaudible.

"What, Bea?" I ask.

Again Bea shields her face and whispers just as inaudibly. She repeats this a few times until finally I hear "What do you think of A-I-D-S?"

"Do you mean AIDS?" I ask.

"Oh, is that the name? I thought you just used the letters. So what do you think of it? And whisper. I don't want the kids to hear."

Charles is talking to Bea's husband, Jeff. Mike is climbing my legs and whining to be picked up. Adam and Erik are trying to trip each other. Bea's kids are clowning around, too. The last thing I feel like doing is discussing a deadly disease in whispers. And considering the fracas being made by the two families' boys, I doubt they'll pick up what we say unless we shout. Still, I know how nervous Bea gets.

"I don't know, Bea," I say. "I guess I haven't given it much thought. NHF claims the CDC is reassuring them, and besides, who knows anything about these three guys who came down with it? For all we know, they could be gay or IV drug users. There's no law saying that hemophiliacs are immune to homosexuality or drug habits."

"You know, Elaine, I hadn't even thought of that. I'll bet there is something odd about these three patients. I mean it's not like there are a lot of hemophiliacs getting sick."

——————

December 21, 1982. The NHF recommends that clotting-factor concentrates not be given to newborns and children "through age four," people newly diagnosed with hemophilia, and those with mild hemophilia. But "at this time the NHF AIDS Task Force does not recommend a change in treatment to those who have received concentrates in therapy. And, by all means, one should not withhold the use of clotting factor therapy when needed."

January 13, 1983. In *The New England Journal of Medicine,* Dr. Jane F. Desforges writes, "Patients receiving lyophilized commercial concentrates of factor VIII appeared more likely than those receiving cryoprecipitate to have abnormalities of T-cell subpopulations. In view of this finding, current modes of treatment must be scrutinized." Dr. Desforges concludes, "Unfortunately, the data are consistent with a greater potential for AIDS in the population treated with concentrate. Physicians involved in the care of hemophiliacs must now be alert to this risk. Preventing the complications of the present treatment may have to take precedence over preventing the complications of hemophilia itself."

February 1983. Dr. Luc Montagnier believes he has found the virus that causes AIDS. Dr. Robert Gallo is working on the same virus in the United States. (That AIDS is caused by a virus was accepted by the medical and scientific community long before the announcement, in the spring of 1984, that the AIDS virus had been jointly discovered by Dr. Gallo and Dr. Montagnier. The only question had been, Which virus?)

May 11, 1983. The National Hemophilia Foundation continues to urge patients to use clotting factor, even though the CDC had informed the NHF in January that half the hemophilia population demonstrated abnormal T-cell function and was expected to develop AIDS. In addition, the NHF expresses concern "that public media coverage of AIDS is causing some patients to abandon appropriate use of blood products, because they fear contracting AIDS. The NHF AIDS Task Force considers this to be an inappropriate response and urges hemophiliacs to maintain the use of clotting factor."

May 1983. Dr. Aledort of the National Hemophilia Foundation gives hemophiliacs the following advice regarding AIDS: "Lead as normal a life as possible. . . . There is no evidence to support that AIDS is transmitted in either cryoprecipitate or concentrate, although it is possible."

August 23, 1983. The NHF addresses the AIDS concerns of the hemophilia population in the *Hemophilia Information Exchange.* To the question "What are the causes?" the NHF answers, "The cause of AIDS is unknown. There are several theories, but none have been proven. The most widely held theory presently is that it is caused by a virus that attacks the immune cell." To the question "How does one get it?" the NHF answers, "This, too, is unknown, since the cause is unknown. There are some data, however, that suggest that it may be transmitted from infected individuals through blood and blood products and intimate contact with certain body secretions." Question: "Is it fatal?" Answer: "The immune deficiency itself is not fatal. Persons who develop the disorder, however, are susceptible to a number of infections. These so-called opportunistic infections are often fatal."

The CDC's *Morbidity and Mortality Weekly Report* for the week preceding this mailing indicated that 1,922 Americans had been stricken with AIDS. In Randy Shilts's *And the Band Played On,* the description of "often fatal" is more specific: "Although only 39 percent of the total caseload was dead, the new figures did not offer a hopeful prognosis. Of all the people diagnosed with AIDS on or before July 26, 1982, at least two-thirds were dead. Few survived among the people who had suffered from the disease two years before."

To the question "Can one do anything to minimize the risk of AIDS?" the NHF advises, "Balanced diet, and appropriate rest, etc. may be valuable in reducing the likelihood of AIDS." There is also the reassurance that "there is no evidence that AIDS is associated with any specific blood product or manufacturer." Finally, "Hemophiliacs are urged not to withhold treatment if it is medically indicated. At the present time there is no specific evidence to warrant changing the use of Factor VIII or Factor IX."

November 2, 1983. In the *Hemophilia Information Exchange*, hemophiliacs are told, "NHF REAFFIRMS POSITION THAT PRODUCT RECALL SHOULD NOT CHANGE USE OF CLOTTING FACTOR."

December 2, 1983. The CDC notes that twenty-one cases of AIDS have been diagnosed in hemophilia patients.

January 24, 1984. "NHF REAFFIRMS POSITION THAT PRODUCT WITHDRAWAL SHOULD NOT CHANGE USE OF CLOTTING FACTOR."

February 3, 1984. The NHF informs its members that "in the medical and scientific community there are different points of view on this topic, but all agree that *if* sexual partners of hemophiliacs are at increased risk for AIDS, *this risk is remote.*"

My friend Andrea sits in her wheelchair at a podium on the statehouse steps. It is July 1995. She sobs as she tells the story of her husband, a hemophiliac who died of AIDS. The pain is written all over her tear-streaked face. She fears for her daughter, an only child. Her daughter lost a father to AIDS. Now she must lose a mother to AIDS. Andrea was infected by the virus that causes AIDS before her husband was diagnosed with the disease.

April 1986. In the *Hemophilia Information Exchange,* the question is asked, "What is the risk of a person with hemophilia getting AIDS?" The NHF answers, "At the present time, less than 1% of the estimated population of 20,000 persons with hemophilia in the United States have contracted AIDS. While the number of persons with hemophilia with AIDS has increased, the total number of cases is still relatively small in the total population." Elsewhere in this publication, however, four years and three months after the first documented cases of heterosexual transmission of AIDS were reported by the CDC (one case was a spouse of a hemophiliac), the NHF finally admits the risks of sexual transmission of HIV from an infected hemophiliac to an uninfected partner. Two years later, the hemophilia community would be told that the rate of transmission of HIV from infected hemophiliacs to their spouses ranges from 10 to 25 percent.

I am admiring my friend Carmen's sable waist-length hair. Even when it's tied back, stray wisps escape to frame her clear, almost luminous face. Carmen and I are stretched barefoot across the beds in her hotel room in Colorado, where we are attending a conference of the Women's Outreach Network of NHF. We are watching a thunderstorm outside the window and pitying the women in our group who went sightseeing. The lightning bounces from mountaintop to mountaintop.

There's a certain thrill in watching lightning strike and knowing you are safe, invulnerable to the sudden disaster it can bring. Carmen rarely feels safe and invulnerable.

We are growing hungrier by the minute as we wait for Cynthia to arrive. Our friend Cynthia has no sense of time. As we joke about Cynthia, giddiness strikes. Whether it's the weather or the hunger, we can't tell. For a few moments, we're no longer two full-grown women burdened with too much responsibility and too much sorrow. We're a couple of teenagers at a pajama party.

So it comes as no surprise when Carmen, totally out of character, rolls onto her back and shouts, "Oh, you didn't know my Charlie. Every time he walked into the room, I wanted to jump all over his body. I was passionately, madly in love with him."

This is a side of Carmen I haven't seen before—the carefree, impulsive girl, full of love and joy.

Carmen married Charlie, and within five years they had two chil-
dren. "Both planned and both adored," says Carmen. "Charlie had a
good job. I was staying home with the children, which I loved." Then
something happened. Charlie, a hemophiliac, complained to his
hematologist about some problems he was having.

Charlie was tested for HIV. The results were positive. Within hours
of receiving the results, Carmen was in the hemophilia center de-
manding to be tested. She, too, was positive. Their children were neg-
ative.

Charlie is dead, and Carmen is angry. She must plan for her chil-
dren's future, a future as orphans.

In April 1986, nearly two years after clinical trials of HIV-antibody testing documented it and five years after many physicians and scientists suspected it, the NHF finally announced that "the AIDS virus is quite sensitive to heat-treatment processes to treat concentrates." It appears to be more than coincidental that this announcement was made in the same month and year that the first trustworthy virally inactivated factor VIII product was licensed to Bayer. The product, Koate HS, was heat-treated in solution at sixty degrees Celsius for ten hours, just as the Behringwerke product was nearly a decade before and much the way human albumin was in 1945.

Many hemophiliacs seriously question the NHF's stewardship of the hemophilia community in the 1980s. They question the loyalties and priorities of an organization that not only failed to advocate a safe treatment but also recklessly encouraged the use of a lethal treatment. They wonder whether funding received from the clotting-factor manufacturers influenced statements made by the NHF.

According to evidence introduced in *Cross v. Cutter Biological et al.*, a hemophilia-HIV lawsuit filed in Louisiana:

> Armour expected more than simple appreciation for its generous contributions, as indicated by the following language: "Armour wants a visible product that can be identified in return for their

support.... Armour wanted control over NHF publications and for $36,000.00 a year and numerous other enticements, that control was obtained...."

Similar Cutter documents ... indicate a similar relationship between Cutter and the National Hemophilia Foundation: "In addition to annual contributions of at least $30,000.00, Cutter goes so far as to provide insurance for the NHF's annual meeting.... In return for their contributions, Cutter was given the rights to exclusive control of the NHF publications program.... Having gained control over the governing body of that organization as well as its educational materials and publications, these pharmaceutical companies were able to continually disseminate misleading information and thereby convince the hemophiliacs nationwide that their product was safe and pure and that they should continue to infuse.

In 1993, Congress instigated an investigation of the events and decisions that led to the transmission of HIV through blood products in the 1980s. The Public Health Service assigned this responsibility to the Institute of Medicine, an independent agency chartered by the National Academy of Sciences. A fourteen-member committee led by Dr. Harold C. Sox, Jr., of the Dartmouth College Medical School spent two years analyzing the information. Regarding the NHF, the Institute of Medicine concluded that "the financial relationship between the NHF and the blood products industry seriously compromised NHF's credibility."

It is only fair to acknowledge that the NHF has been undergoing a major transformation in the 1990s. It has developed new programs to increase peer involvement in the organization, replaced its executive director, and issued strict conflict-of-interest guidelines. Beginning in late 1992, the NHF's Medical and Scientific Advisory Council and the board of directors of the NHF passed resolutions indicating a reaffirmation of the NHF's responsibility to hemophiliacs as its highest priority. However, members are understandably dismayed by the NHF's continuing acceptance of large contributions from the plasma-fractionating industry.

In the 1980s, some of the leaders of the NHF may have deliberately attempted to deceive the membership. In all probability, a greater number fell victim to wishful thinking–a need to deny the reality of the AIDS catastrophe. It should be remembered that some of the so-called ogres within this organization contracted HIV from their own clotting-factor concentrate. Some have died. Others were parents of hemophilic children. They have either lost their children or they are watching them slowly wither away.

CHAPTER 6

*In the
Shadow of
AIDS*

IN LATE 1986, I TOLD A MIDWESTERN TELEVISION NEWS REPORTER
that I was not concerned about my children developing AIDS. Having been reassured by my hematologist that an HIV-positive test result meant only that the virus had passed through a patient's system
and he had developed antibodies to it and, therefore, immunity, I
wasn't even interested in knowing my children's HIV status. I told
the reporter, "As a mother of sons with hemophilia, my greatest fear
is that my children will be hit by a car. They stand a greater chance
of dying in an accident than of AIDS." To this day, memories of tap-
ing that television program haunt me.

A few months later, on a bitterly cold February morning, I received a telephone call from the New Jersey State Police. Mike's
school van had turned over on the interstate, and he was being
transported to the Trauma Center at Cooper Hospital–University
Medical Center in Camden. He suffered a depressed skull fracture
that badly tore the dura mater, the protective covering of the brain.
Eventually a craniotomy was required, in which hundreds of bone
splinters were removed from his brain, and tissue from his abdomen was grafted onto the torn and punctured dura mater.

The complications from Mike's accident necessitated years of re-
habilitation. All the speech therapy my little deaf child with a cleft
palate had endured was wasted. His ability to speak was destroyed

by the injury. He was left partially paralyzed, visually impaired, and deeply traumatized. In addition, Mike developed diabetes insipidus as a result of damage to his pituitary gland.

Diabetes insipidus is a totally different disorder from diabetes mellitus (sugar diabetes). Diabetes insipidus renders the body incapable of regulating fluid loss. From the time of his accident on, Mike was constantly at risk of becoming dehydrated. Eventually he required daily injections with DDAVP, a synthetic pituitary hormone.

Somehow I deluded myself with the belief that Mike's accident validated what I had told the television reporter. Accidents were my greatest concern, not AIDS. I clung desperately to this philosophy when, seven months after Mike's accident, in August 1987, Cubby was hospitalized with bacteremia.

Cubby's pediatrician called me into the hallway outside the hospital room. Without preamble, she said, "Mrs. DePrince, Cubby has AIDS. I would like to test him for HIV." At that moment, I felt as though she had punched me in the chest. Terror was my immediate emotional reaction. Cubby was only six years old. I adored him. I couldn't conceive of him suffering. I couldn't imagine his dying. I couldn't imagine coping with the cruelty and the ostracism that was bound to become a part of this cheerful, friendly child's life. I knew that if Cubby had AIDS, the chances were high that at least one of my other children also had AIDS. And in 1987 no drugs were available to treat a six-year-old child with AIDS.

Why subject Cubby and his brothers to discrimination and hatred? Why live in sadness and fear when there was no hope available? Why make him vulnerable to legislation that might force him to suffer alone? (There was talk among politicians of isolating AIDS patients on the Hawaiian island of Molokai.)

"No," I told the pediatrician. "Care for him as though he has AIDS if you like, but don't test him. Don't make him a potential victim of fear and discrimination. If a drug becomes available to treat him, then test him, but not yet."

The pediatrician insisted on testing him. I argued against it. The argument became heated and ugly. Finally she told me, "If you won't agree to testing, then I refuse to treat him."

"Fine, good-bye. You're off the case. You're fired," I retorted. Holding back my tears, I peeked into Cubby's room. He was lying still, curled up under his covers. "Sweetie pie, are you OK?" I asked.

"Mommy, why were you and the doctor having an argument in the hall? Was it something bad about me?"

"We didn't agree on something, Cubs. She wanted to run some tests that I didn't approve of. She got a bit grumpy and loud. Don't worry about her. I'm going to find a quieter doctor for you, but first I want to go to the cafeteria for a cup of coffee. Can you rest while I'm gone?"

Cubby gave me a long stranglehold hug and a faceful of kisses. I could barely contain my emotions. After a dozen good-byes, he let me leave. I hurried to the telephone outside the pediatrics wing and called Charles. He was stunned as I sobbed the story to him. He agreed with my decision to protect Cubby for as long as we could, and he helped me locate a pediatrician who understood our predicament.

From mid-1987 to mid-1988, Cubby didn't appear to be sicker than the average child. Without knowing for sure what his HIV status was, Charles and I worked hard to convince ourselves that the first pediatrician was wrong. In May 1988, when I brought Teddy, Cubby, and Mike to the hematologist for their annual hemophilia evaluation and it was discovered that Cubby had a low-grade fever, I told myself that he had gotten overheated playing in the waiting room. But when the records showed that he hadn't grown or gained weight in the past year, I knew he was in trouble. The final blow came from his laboratory test results. He was anemic. His white cell count was low and out of sync, and his platelet count was dangerously low.

Dr. Susan Travis, the children's hematologist and a neighbor, understood the possible discrimination we would encounter if the results of their HIV tests fell into the wrong hands. She suggested that I bring the boys for anonymous HIV testing by the Camden County Department of Health. Three weeks later I received the test results for all three of our younger sons. They were all positive, and Cubby's T-4 (also referred to as CD4) count was so low he was considered even then to be severely immune depressed.

When a family with children adopts another child, the social worker always asks, "Why do you want to do this?" I had a special answer to this question: I wanted a large family; I was willing to put up with all the inconveniences and sacrifices. "It's my dream that in my old age I'll reign over a Thanksgiving Day table filled with my sons, their wives, and numerous grandchildren," I told the adoption workers. I wanted to know that through my family, I had not just taken from life but had given back as well.

On Thanksgiving Day 1988, as we joined hands to give thanks, I felt such pain and anger. I had asked for only one thing out of life. I hadn't asked for wealth and fame. Mine was a simple enough request, but it wasn't going to be fulfilled. As I looked at the faces of my five beautiful sons, I was filled with anguish. I wondered which face would be absent from our table the next year and the next year and the year after that.

From July of 1988 on, our family lived in the shadow of AIDS. All our decisions revolved around the status of the children's immune systems, yet we were determined to make life as normal as possible. We wanted to fit as much happiness and joy as we could into what for our children might be very short lives.

We had always traveled north or south on our many vacations, though our boys had clamored to travel west. In the summer of 1988, aware that we could not know which vacation would be their last, we decided to take the children on a mammoth trip west. We spread out maps and told each child that he could pick any spot he wanted, and we would go there. Some of their choices would not have been ours, but we honored them nonetheless. Erik chose Dinosaur National Monument. Adam chose Grand Teton National Park. Mike chose Yellowstone National Park. Cubby chose Mount Rushmore National Memorial. Teddy, who had just read Laura Ingalls Wilder's *Little House on the Prairie,* wanted nothing more than to cross the prairies and find a buffalo chip.

We panned for gold, viewed dinosaur fossils and caves. We saw bison, moose, elk, pronghorn antelope, mule deer, coyotes, and eagles. We rented a pontoon boat and traveled along the Flaming Gorge in Utah, swam in the Great Salt Lake, walked on volcanic tableland, and witnessed a mighty forest fire. Cubby claimed to see the yellow brick road to Oz in the sunset on the horizon of Kansas. Much to his delight, Teddy found plenty of buffalo chips. He carefully wrapped one in aluminum foil to take home. He planned to dazzle his third-grade classmates back in New Jersey.

Charles and I saved our choice until last. On the way home, we camped for several days on the northern peninsula of Michigan. With the sandy shores of Lake Superior less than fifty feet from our camper, Charles and I relaxed and watched our five boys working together to build a complex system of towns, castles, roads, and waterways in the sand, assisted by our magnificent digging machine, Stripe, the dog.

Though the effects of HIV were more apparent in laboratory reports than in the children in 1988, knowing what I knew placed a burden on me that made this vacation far less carefree than our trip to Nova Scotia had been. After traveling across the country to see the Rocky Mountains I burst into tears at the first sight of them. I cried inconsolably as my family tried to comfort me. "What's wrong, Mommy? What's wrong? Why are you crying?"

"They're nothing but rocks," I cried.

"That's why they're called the Rocky Mountains," everybody chorused.

The sight of bare rock reminded me of death. I wanted to see the lush, life-affirming greenery of my beloved Appalachians. Everything about the West reminded me of death—especially Dinosaur National Monument and Mount Rushmore. I had wanted to enjoy myself. I didn't want to think about time and mortality, but the starkness and emptiness of the surroundings and the reminders of the people and bison cruelly slaughtered and gone forever from the land drew my thoughts back again and again to the future deaths of my children.

In May of 1988, when his T-4 count was still a bit over 200, I began fighting to get Cubby treatment with AZT (Retrovir), the first anti-

HIV drug produced. It was available for adults at that time, but not for children unless they had lost 10 percent of their body weight. The pediatric infectious-disease specialist was waiting for Cubby's weight to drop as I was stuffing him to keep his weight up. Cubby wasn't losing weight, but he wasn't growing and gaining weight, as a young child should.

In January 1989, Cubby was forty-five inches tall and weighed only forty-three pounds. He was sick constantly, and his T-4 count was only 62, yet he was denied the drug because he didn't meet the criteria established for pediatric patients. He still hadn't lost 10 percent of his weight. Criteria for kids should have been based on T-4 counts, as they were for adults. The kids were always the losers in this disease. They were denied the newest drugs because the FDA was concerned about the effect the drugs would have on growing bodies. Children like Cubby weren't growing, and without the AZT they were going to die, but when it came to children and AIDS, the FDA had its own brand of logic.

One year after Cubby's first T-4 count, when he was nearly eight years old, his weight had finally dropped the requisite 10 percent. He weighed only thirty-nine pounds, so AZT was prescribed for him. By that time, however, he had virtually no T-4 cells left. They never returned. Taking AZT just became a useless daily exercise in toxicity.

Despite his grim prospects, Cubby struggled on, sick more often than not. He was sustained by his overwhelmingly positive personality, high spirits, and faith in Mommy's ability to make everything right.

By this time, we had told all our children the truth. We needed everyone to pull together as a team. Life might get hard for all of them. AIDS is a frightening illness whose victims are greatly discriminated against, and Cubby had not been very good at keeping a secret.

On December 22, 1989, Cubby was sick with pneumonia. At our hemophilia center, I was taken aside by the social worker, who told me it was time to decide whether or not the family wanted Cubby to die at home. Though he probably would survive his current infection, with no immune system remaining, he couldn't possibly survive for long. That decision weighed heavily on my mind as I took Cubby home with me that afternoon. Arrangements were made with a home-care company for the medications and equipment he would need.

We had a sixty-five-mile ride home on the heavily trafficked New Jersey Turnpike. Despite severe hives, a high fever, and constant coughing, Cubby perked up when we approached the Molly Pitcher Rest Stop near exit 8. "Are you up to it, Cubs?" I asked. He beamed back at me.

I wrapped Cubby in a heavy blanket and lifted him into his wheelchair. Though gray faced and exhausted, he was excited to be visiting his friends. Over the years of traveling to and from hemophilia centers, Cubby had developed friendships with all the waitresses and managers at this rest stop. The women at Bob's Big Boy restaurant were some of the kindest, most helpful people I encountered throughout the period of my children's illnesses. They knew that Cubby had AIDS, yet they hugged him, kissed him, and fussed over him. They brought him joy and often helped me to unwind after a tough clinic appointment.

That night, I had to broach the subject of death with Charles. He and I handled things differently. I worried excessively, and Charles just put problems out of his mind. To him, HIV and AIDS were problems to be overcome just as easily as any other problems were overcome. Since I was the the family's primary caregiver for hemophilia, and since the children always did well, Charles just assumed I would somehow keep them well despite AIDS. Though Charles knew that people died from the complications arising from AIDS, he was stunned when forced to confront the fact that our Cubby, the child who had chosen the name Charles John DePrince, Jr., in honor of his adoptive father, would die of this disease.

As difficult as facing death was for Charles, it was doubly so for Adam and Erik. They were teenagers, and teenagers feel immortal. Death happens only to old people and people they don't know. They cried and protested–"This can't be true. I don't want him to die.

Don't let him die. Mom, call somebody up, and locate a cure. You always find a way. Dad, tell her. Tell her to find a way to make him well." Dad had always paid the bills and fixed broken objects. Mom had always helped with homework and made the children well. That was the way things worked in our family. I felt as though I had failed in my duty.

I explained to Adam and Erik that I couldn't make Cubby well, but I was determined that when his time came to die, he would do so without fear. I wanted Cubby to be able to talk about death as though it were no more frightening than being born. That night our family embarked on a spiritual endeavor that we never strayed from, even when we were swamped by the physical strains of caring for children with AIDS.

At midnight on Christmas Eve, when everybody else had fallen asleep, I was still up with Cubby, giving him medicine and breathing treatments. His mouth and throat were covered with painful herpes blisters. His chest hurt with every breath. I thought bitterly how visions of sugar plums should be dancing in his head at this very moment. Suddenly Cubby started to cry. He asked, "Mommy, am I going to die?"

Christmas carols, playing softly in the next room, added a surreal quality to the moment. To this day, I cannot hear those songs without thinking of Cubby's question and my answer. "If you mean, will you die from this pneumonia and this herpes infection, then the answer is no. But I will not lie to you. . . . If you mean, will AIDS cause you to die while you are still a child, the answer is yes."

Cubby stopped crying. He wiped his tears and never really cried again. He thanked me and began to make plans for his short little future. He had so much to do, and so little time in which to do it. His plans weren't wishes for fun and adventure. He didn't ask for special trips to magical places or visits with his favorite celebrities. Instead, he wished to leave his mark in the world. He wanted to write books that wouldn't be forgotten. He wanted to spread a message of hope and love. He wanted to help the homeless, the hungry, and other suffering children.

Cubby did all this. He appeared on television nearly a dozen times. He spoke of living the life he had rather than of longing for the unattainable. He raised money for homeless children and children with AIDS. He made sandwiches for homeless men and women who slept on steam vents in Philadelphia, and he saved his allowance and gifts of money from his great-aunts to buy a Thanksgiving dinner for a large family that had just emigrated from Vietnam. He prepared educational materials for AIDS-awareness programs and wrote children's books as well as more than two hundred pages of memoirs.

To fully appreciate Cubby's efforts, it's helpful to follow him through a complete day. At first, I kept a log of each of his days, but this became too strenuous for me, physically and emotionally. I do have a log of Thanksgiving 1992, however, because I was certain it would be Cubby's last Thanksgiving Day.

5:13 A.M. Cubby wakes up with pain in the side of his chest and shoulder. His temperature is 91.4 degrees. He's shivering. He's gray and peaked. I give him codeine with warm chocolate milk. I put him in the hospital bed downstairs. I put the heating pad on his shoulder. We chat awhile, and he falls asleep holding my hand. I sleep in the recliner next to his bed.

8:00 A.M. I flush Cubby's heparin lock, a catheter in the vein of his arm, and run an Amikin IV drip. He is taking this drug because he has an always fatal opportunistic infection called MAI [*Mycobacterium avium-intracellulare*]. He has had it for over two years. It usually kills in six to ten months. How Cubby has managed to survive this long with MAI is a tribute to his spirit. Cubby sleeps through the IV and I begin to prepare stuffing for the turkey.

9:00 A.M. Cubby wakes up as I disconnect the Amikin IV. He's happy, excited, and pain free. He eats ½ slice of toast, 2 teaspoons of applesauce, and drinks a cup of chocolate milk. He takes Zovirax for a systemic herpes infection; ddC, an anti-HIV drug; and Megace, a synthetic steroid that stimulates his appetite and seems to supress his AIDS-associated central-nervous-system symptoms.

9:30 A.M. Cubby washes up, dresses in one of his favorite neon outfits, brushes his teeth, and rinses his mouth with Peridex, a treatment for his AIDS-associated gingivitis. Then Cubby sucks on a Mycelex Troche to control oral thrush.

10:00 A.M. Cubby writes in his memoirs and chats with me from the hospital bed in the adjoining family room as I prepare Thanksgiving dinner in the kitchen.

10:20 A.M. Cubby convinces me to let him make the cranberry sauce. He climbs on a chair, and Charles holds him steady while I hold the pot. Cubby adds a pound of cranberries, a cup of sugar, and a cup of water. Then he stirs vigorously, waiting for the moment when . . . "The cranberries are popping, Dad. That means any second it's going to thicken. Look, it's thickening. Yay! A success."

10:45 A.M. Cubby sits in his reclining wheelchair in the kitchen. Everybody is pitching in with the dinner preparations, and he doesn't want to miss the excitement.

11:00 A.M. He takes Biaxin, Mycobutin, and ciprofloxacin, part of the heavy antibiotic regimen to keep his MAI at bay. He has a snack of two crackers.

11:15 A.M. Adam, who has been away at college, helps Cubby into his snowsuit and wraps him in a blanket. Adam plans to take Cubby for a ride in his wagon. They are deep in conversation. They've missed each other. Adam is home only for the weekend.

11:45 A.M. Adam brings Cubby back into the house. Cubby has a headache. He thinks that he is going to throw up. He does throw up. I take his temperature. It is 104.5. I give him a Tylenol, put an ice pack on his head, and put him in the hospital bed. He falls asleep immediately. Adam cries. I try to comfort him, but he keeps asking, "Why didn't you tell me he had gotten so much worse?" Adam sits by Cubby's bedside, studying.

1:00 P.M. I wake up Cubby. He is drenched in sweat. The fever is down. He's hungry. He sits in the wheelchair and eats a tiny piece of homemade pie, which he helped me bake the night before. He takes his Suprax, an antibiotic for a permanent sinus infection; his

Diflucan, an antifungal to prevent oral thrush from spreading throughout his gastrointestinal system; and Myambutol. He changes from his soggy outfit into another set of neon-colored clothes and settles back into bed. I assign him the job of making place cards for the dinner table. Erik, the family artist, helps him. Together they draw and color turkeys, pumpkins, Pilgrim hats, and peace pipes.

2:00 P.M. Cubby insists on kneading the bread dough with me. He tires after getting thoroughly covered with flour. He decides to rest in his wheelchair and watch me.

2:45 P.M. Charles has dusted the flour from Cubby's clothes and put him back to bed. Cubby puts Christmas carols on his tape player, and we all sing. Cubby, Teddy, and I, the singers of the family, harmonize.

3:15 P.M. Cubby decides to read his novel. Mike brings his new Isaac Asimov science fiction and sits on the recliner next to him. Both boys read quietly while the other three continue to help me in the kitchen.

4:00 P.M. Cubby has fallen asleep. Mike is still reading. I flush Cubby's heparin lock and drip the Amikin.

4:15 P.M. The Sloans arrive. Leanne, Rick, and their sixteen-year-old daughter, Nicole, are celebrating Thanksgiving with us. Cubby is awakened by the voices. He's perky and excited.

5:00 P.M. I disconnect Cubby's IV while he shows the Sloans the place cards he made. Dinner is ready. We join hands and give our individual thanks. When it comes to Cubby's turn, he says, "Thank you God for letting me live another year."

5:15 P.M. Cubby is actually eating something–turkey and home-made bread. He takes his Zovirax and ddC with dinner.

6:30 P.M. He is going strong. Cubby plays Scattergories and Balderdash with the adults while the kids are off playing video games in Mike's room. We laugh at Cubby's lame attempt to come up with a definition for some esoteric word. He has given us "a fungus that scurries." "OK, Cubs. Sounds like you're tired." Cubby laughs and agrees to take a nap. He thinks that he ate too much, and his stomach hurts. I place the heating pad on his tummy, more for psychological comfort than anything else. Cubby naps.

9:00 P.M. Cubby wakes up for dessert. He's in high spirits again and ready to join his brothers and Nicole in their games.

10:00 P.M. After a lot of laughing and clowning around, Cubby has too much pain. I give him codeine with chocolate milk and tuck him into the hospital bed. He falls asleep instantly, oblivious to the noise around him.

11:00 P.M. I wake Cubby up for his Biaxin, Mycobutin, and ciprofloxacin. He gets up to say good-bye to our company.

12:00 midnight I give Cubby his factor VIII, then drip the Amikin. He's wide awake, and since it's a holiday, we all decide to watch a movie that Charles has rented. The movie is punctuated by Cubby's continuous comments on the characterization and plots. Adam and Erik keep saying, "Shhh, Cubby. Cubby, be quiet. Gag him, Mom." I ignore all of them. This has been going on for years. Cubby can't keep quiet during a movie, and rather than ignore him, the older boys encourage him with their protests.

1:00 A.M. I administer Neupogen by IV, to stimulate his bone marrow.

1:45 A.M. The movie is done. Everybody heads off to bed. Cubby still has medication to take. He eats another slice of apple pie and drinks about 4 ounces of grape juice. He takes his Zovirax and ddC. He brushes his teeth and rinses with Peridex. He sucks on his final Mycelex Troche. He knows that he can't go to bed with something in his mouth, so he drags out the process of sucking the lozenge.

2:00 A.M. Cubby is really taking advantage of his Mycelex Troche. He thinks that we don't know that. Neither Charles nor I have any intention of rushing him along. He's feeling good and is talkative, as usual. He has decided that this has been a "splendid Thanksgiving." Cubby wonders if the Vietnamese family enjoyed their Thanksgiving dinner. Pencil and paper in hand, he begins to plan his fund-raising and shopping expedition for the Christmas gifts that he wants to buy for the children in the homeless shelter. Last of all he begs for a few minutes to write in his memoirs upstairs in his room. We tuck him into the recliner. He falls asleep while writing in his memoirs.

3:00 A.M. After a late-night snack and a few moments together, Charles and I head off to bed. We check on all of the little boys.

Cubby's light is on, and he has left a note lying on his stomach: "Please, remember to give me an extra kiss before you go to bed."

———————

By Thanksgiving 1992, while our family was trying to cope with Cubby's end-stage AIDS, Mike had advanced AIDS, and Teddy's T-4 count was below 200. Mike had contracted measles in March of 1992 and suffered progressive neurological decline afterward. All our efforts to rehabilitate him following his 1987 accident were thwarted by the progress of AIDS. He was on nearly as many medications as Cubby.

Charles was solely responsible for earning a living during that time because the children's declining health prevented me from returning to my teaching career. As a result, the bulk of the physical, emotional, and spiritual care of our family fell upon my shoulders. Every night, Adam would call from college and inquire about his brothers' health. Every night, I had to determine just how much I should tell him.

Adam had graduated from high school with honors in 1991. He had been elected to the Senior Hall of Fame, an honor for students who contributed notably to the betterment of the school. In college, he made the dean's list every semester. He was a promising computer science major, with plans for graduate school. He had to deal with his own medical problems, especially with Tourette syndrome, a hereditary neurological disorder that has complicated his life. The accompanying tics were often so intense and painful that Cubby once said, "When I watch Adam and think about the courage that it takes to make something of himself knowing that everyone is staring at him because of his tics, I think that it is actually easier having AIDS." Knowing that Adam's tics were exacerbated by stress, at Cubby's request, I often withheld information about the progression of his AIDS.

Erik was a senior in high school that Thanksgiving. He was a talented cartoonist, and he was trying to make plans for his future. This troubled him because he knew that he was planning for a fu-

ture in which Cubby would not exist. Other high school seniors in
Erik's school looked forward eagerly to June of 1993. Erik did not.
The thought of time passing so swiftly and of losing his brother was
too frightening.

Teddy was in junior high school. He was doted upon by his teachers and popular with his peers. He was a talented singer and active
in theater. Cubby was one year younger than Teddy. Mike was one
year older than Teddy. Cubby and Mike were withering before his
eyes. He knew that he had the same disease and that with his T-4
cell count under 200, he might join them in their steady decline at
any time. Yet he remained focused on achievement—on living in the
present as much as possible.

Mike and Cubby spent every day at home. Mike was often content
just to sit by Cubby's side while his brother slept. When awake,
Cubby was Mike's voice. Mike usually communicated with us by
writing on a pad of paper, but Cubby claimed to know what Mike
wanted just by looking at him. I often thought that Cubby made re-
quests for Mike based on what he himself wanted. One afternoon,
however, Mike looked over at Cubby, and Cubby turned to me and
said, "Mom, Mike would like a grilled-cheese sandwich." I had detected no sign of communication between the boys, so I asked
Cubby what he wanted to eat, and he told me a slice of toast and
jelly. I picked up a pad of paper and wrote, "Mike, do you want to eat
lunch? What do you want?" Mike wrote in response, "Yes, lunch—a
grilled-cheese sandwich."

By New Year's Day of 1993, some of Cubby's more uncomfortable
medical treatments, like the Amikin IV, had been discontinued.
They just weren't working. A do-not-resuscitate letter from his
AIDS treatment center was hidden behind a picture frame in the living room. Cubby brought up the topic of death frequently. He believed in God, guardian angels, and heaven. He felt secure with
dying. He once explained to me, "I'm not scared of dying. I'm just
nervous about going someplace strange. It's the feeling I had when
I went to the Hole in the Wall Gang camp for the first time. I'm not
sure what to expect."

Cubby wanted to spend as much time in my presence as possible during those last months. I often took him with me, even on routine errands. It was an inconvenient procedure, having to carry an extra factor VIII case, a case full of medication, and a reclining wheelchair, but the inconvenience was minor compared with the pleasure Cubby and I got from these outings. On the rare occasions when I left the house without him, I would come home to find him wearing my satin ponytail holder on his wrist. He explained, "When you go out, I always worry that something bad will happen to you. If I wear your scrunchy I feel as though you are safe. If something ever happened to you, I wouldn't be able to live one more day because you take such good care of me. I know that it's you keeping me alive. I love you so much I'd want to be with you in heaven."

Through all these painful days, life was never dark and dreary. On the contrary, our days were filled with fun and laughter. Mike and Cubby had a teacher, Bernice, who had been with us for a few years. Each weekday during the school year she spent hours with us—far more hours than she was being paid for. But then she didn't spend all that time teaching. She visited and usually had lunch with us. Cubby would take orders and call the take-out service for delivery.

One day when Cubby and Bernice were deep in conversation about a tabloid report on aliens, Cubby placed his hand on Bernice's arm, looked into her eyes, and said, "Bernice, I wish you were my grandmother."

Bernice had indeed at some point crossed the line between teacher and grandmother. She often brought treasures and treats for the boys. She telephoned them and sent postcards when she was on vacation. She returned with souvenirs for them and even for me. She began bringing Halloween surprises by late September. Christmas surprises arrived tucked in her tote bag by the first of December—even though she is Jewish. Cubby wanted to celebrate Hanukkah with Bernice, so she brought him his own Hanukkah menorah and brightly colored candles.

Joanie, a part-time special education student in her twenties, was originally hired as Mike's attendant. Eventually Cubby considered her his "best friend who was a girl." His best friend who was a boy was Scott, and his girlfriend (as in romantic interest) was Brooke, one of his camp counselors, who visited regularly. Mike first thought that Joanie was a nurse, and eventually he decided that because she was around so much, we must have adopted her. He thought of her as his big sister.

Joanie and I often took the boys to the mall, where Mike indulged in video games and Cubby bought gifts. We made many trips to the movie theater on weekday afternoons. We had frequent visitors, and Cubby held court from his hospital bed in the family room while shy Mike shut himself in his room with his video games.

Cubby developed two passions, writing and art. He began writing his memoirs on the night of September 28, 1992, as a result of a promise that I had made to him on that awful Christmas Eve of 1989. I had promised him that he would not have to worry about always being in imminent danger of dying. I promised him that when he was close to death, I would tell him.

On the afternoon of September 28, I had taken Cubby for a short walk along the Appalachian Trail on Loft Mountain in Virginia. We sat on a large boulder and looked at the farms in the valley below us. The rain had just stopped, and the sun came out, and with it a magnificent rainbow appeared over the valley. It seemed to end at our boulder. I asked Cubby what a rainbow symbolized, and he told me, "A promise." Then I reminded him of the promise I had made to him when he was eight years old. I gently told him that it was likely he wouldn't survive the school year.

Cubby had not cried or complained once about his plight in the three years since I had made that promise. But on this occasion, one tear rolled down his face. He wiped it away and made plans to write his memoirs. He added to them every night thereafter. The memoirs were a secret project, hidden from everyone but his immediate family. He wanted to be remembered and hoped that I would have his work published after his death. He also wanted it to be a gift to those he loved.

Cubby's second passion was color. He loved bright-colored clothes. He wrote his memoirs in ink of various hues. He braided colorful bracelets for friends. But mainly he enjoyed coloring with markers. Erik loved to draw and ink cartoons, but he hated being his own colorist, whereas Cubby's soul soared when he was coloring. So every morning when he went to school, Erik would leave behind a copy of a cartoon he had drawn the night before. These cartoons became the highlight of Cubby's mornings. And once he had completed a coloring job, he excitedly awaited his brother's return from school so he could show him what he had done. Despite Cubby's prognosis, the boys made plans to go into business when they were adults. Erik would major in cartooning in college, and Cubby decided to major in graphic arts.

Cubby and Erik also planned a series of illustrated children's books. First, Cubby wanted Erik to illustrate an excerpt from his memoirs entitled "Visiting Daddy's Plant." He also wanted Erik to illustrate *Cubby, Like a Balloon,* a children's book he was writing. A third project was a children's novel entitled *Electroboy,* for which Cubby had completed several chapters. He and Erik considered turning them into individual books. They were excited about these projects, and they planned to begin work on them the day after Erik graduated from high school.

On June 2, 1993, Joanie and I packed up the boys for the nearly one-hundred-mile ride to Newark, to the AIDS Program at the Children's Hospital of New Jersey, a trip we had been making every month for three years. At one point, this journey had become so arduous that Charles and I had bought a motor home so that the children could be more comfortable. This time they settled into their favorite niches and all of them fell asleep except Cubby. He vomited the whole hundred miles to Newark.

At the clinic, Cubby's doctor looked at his chest X rays and told me that Cubby had developed PCP (*Pneumocystis carinii pneumonia*). Cubby was already in so much pain with MAI infection in all his organs and in his bone marrow that we decided not to put him through the rigorous treatment for PCP. I felt, however, that the final decision regarding a biopsy and treatment should lie with Cubby.

He asked how long he would live without treatment. I told him about one week. He refused treatment but asked that he be permitted to go home. He wanted to die at home, as he had planned. He also wanted me to keep him as free of pain as possible.

Cubby vomited continuously on the way home, but as we approached the Molly Pitcher Rest Stop, he shouted, "Stop." I pulled in, and he explained that he needed to say good-bye to all his good friends who had been so kind to him. As we settled around a table in Bob's Big Boy, Cubby, laboriously, and in obvious pain, climbed out of his wheelchair.

Cubby walked over to each of his favorite waitresses. He hugged each of them and said good-bye. One of the waitresses came over and asked me, "Is he doing what I think he's doing?" I nodded my head, and she began to cry. Though Cubby had no appetite, he ate a small piece of fried chicken to please his friends.

The following week was a nightmare of nausea and pain for Cubby, but he was always gracious. He planned his memorial service and shared his last wishes. He never cried or made demands. He kept apologizing for the inconvenience he was causing me with his constant diarrhea and vomiting. Finally I insisted that he stop apologizing. I told him, "It is a privilege to care for you. You are the most courageous, compassionate, and perfect human being I have ever met. I am honored to have been given you for a son, so let me do a mother's job and clean you up without listening to your apologies."

Cubby smiled weakly and said, "It's been an honor having you for a mother. You have truly been the wind beneath my wings."

Late at night on the eighth of June, I told Cubby that I didn't think he would survive the night. I told him that when he saw a light, he was to follow it to heaven. He asked me whether I would be sad, and I admitted that I would but that I was far sadder watching him suffer. In his typically gracious way, Cubby thanked me because, he admitted, "I'm so tired that I'm ready to die."

Cubby never showed the least bit of panic or fear. When he stopped breathing, he sat up and gestured to me. I asked him whether he saw the light. He nodded yes. Then he laid his head back on the pillow and peacefully died, in his own home, surrounded by his loved ones.

———————

Throughout the years that Cubby lived so precariously with AIDS, Teddy lived more sturdily. AZT became available to him before his T-4 cell count dropped below 100. With the AZT, his T-4 count remained above 100 but seldom crept above the magic number, 200. Above 200 meant that Teddy's chances of staying well were good; below 200 meant that I woke up each morning wondering whether the day had finally dawned when Teddy's health would also decline to the point of no return.

Teddy gave very little thought to the disease when he was younger. His dragons were impulsive behavior and steadily increasing hyperactivity. In the third grade, he was classified as emotionally disturbed. This diagnosis led to his placement in different schools, where his body was often injured by aggressive children, and his spirit was damaged by angry teachers, frustrated by his lack of response to their "behavior-modification" programs. Each day he stepped off the school bus just a bit more forlorn and saddened. He'd ask me, "Mommy, why do I act like that in school? I want to be good, but I can't."

Charles and I decided that enough was enough the year he brought home a thumbprint picture of himself. To make their pictures, the children had put their thumbs on an ink pad and then pressed them onto a piece of paper. They were then instructed to draw a self-portrait on the thumbprint. The picture was supposed to depict each child as he perceived himself. Teddy drew a devil, a devil with a very sad face. His teacher laughed at the picture and told him, "That's you, all right." We knew then that it was time to bring him back to his neighborhood school.

By the time Teddy returned to his own school, he was in the sixth grade. He had poor self-esteem and was still hyperactive. Ironically, it was a health crisis that turned Teddy's life around. His weight and

T-4 cell count dropped. He developed chronic diarrhea, persistent sinusitis, ear infections, and fatigue. He looked skeletal. In order to stimulate his appetite, the doctor prescribed a steroid, Megace.

Not only did Teddy's weight soar with Megace, but he also had a bizarre reaction to the drug. It reduced the negative effect of HIV on his central nervous system so that two weeks after starting the drug he was no longer "emotionally disturbed." He was just a normal eleven-year-old with a very serious medical problem that had caused his brain to go awry. For the first time that Teddy could remember, he liked himself.

The following year, Teddy entered junior high school. His intelligence and sweet personality were finally noticed. His teachers loved him. He made friends. He was popular. In junior high school, he found happiness, but it was a bittersweet happiness because in his soul he was grieving for his brothers. Since his newfound sense of goodness and popularity were so tenuous, however, he hid his grief from everyone at school. He kept a smile pasted on his face because he was afraid that if he cried, acted sad, or showed his anger, nobody would like him.

Cubby's death destroyed Mike. He missed his little brother intensely. At the clinic in Newark, he would look at all the brown babies and write in his notebook, "Boy or girl?" If it was a boy baby, he would write, "Adopt a brown boy baby." Once I wrote, "And what do you want to name an adopted baby?" My heart broke when he answered, "Cubby."

Mike spent hours each day sitting in the recliner, staring at the spot where Cubby's hospital bed used to stand. I didn't have the heart to bring another hospital bed into the house when Mike's health declined and he needed one. Instead, I bought him a water bed, which he found to be wonderfully warm and comfortable.

In hopes of raising Mike's spirits and giving him the will to fight against his disease, I planned a trip to Disney World, a place that Mike thought of as heaven on earth. Our flight was scheduled for

Monday morning, March 14, 1994. In an essay that he wrote in the fall of 1994, Teddy, then a high school freshman, told the story of the weekend preceding Mike's scheduled trip to Disney World in frank and brutal detail:

> It was a sunny Saturday afternoon. Mike was sitting on his bed, watching the weather station. He wanted to know what the weather was going to be like in Orlando, Florida, because he was leaving Monday morning for a trip to Disney World. Mike loved Disney World so much that when he was little he wanted us to call him Mickey Mouse.
>
> I was in the room with him because after the weather we were going to play video games. The map of the United States showed that it was 72 degrees in Orlando. Mike wrote that down in a notebook so he wouldn't forget to tell Mom and Dad.
>
> All of a sudden he arched his back and fell onto the bed. His arms and legs were rigid. He looked scared. I screamed for help and tried to turn him on his side because that was what they do in the television show *Rescue 911* if somebody is having a seizure.
>
> My brother Erik came running into the room. He helped me turn Mike onto his side. He noticed that Mike was turning blue and that he was not breathing. He yelled, "Breathe, Mike, breathe!"
>
> I ran upstairs to call Mom. She came running down. She checked Mike. She said, "He's breathing, but I don't think that he can see anything."
>
> When the seizure didn't stop, Mom called the doctor. Our doctor knew that Mike had end-stage AIDS. That meant that he was close to dying. The doctor told Mom that we could try to treat him at home or bring him to the hospital.
>
> We didn't want to bring him to the hospital because Mike was scared of hospitals. He had made us promise him that we would let him die at home. We all said to Mom, "No, don't take Mike to the hospital. It's not as though the hospital could save his life or anything."
>
> Mom called the doctor back. She told him that we wanted to keep Mike home. The doctor told Mom to give Mike intravenous Valium.

By that time Dad had gotten home from the store. He had gone out earlier to buy Mike new luggage for his trip to Disney World. The luggage was covered with a jungle design and Mike would have loved it, if he could have seen it.

To get the Valium into Mike, Mom had to put in a heparin lock. That is a type of an IV needle that can stay in place for hours, or sometimes for days. For Mom to get the needle into Mike's vein, we all had to hold him down because he was still having a convulsion.

We held Mike down very gently because we didn't want to hurt him. I laid my body over his legs. My brother Adam cradled Mike's head. Erik held Mike's shoulders and Dad held Mike's arms in place.

Mom got Mike's vein with one stick. She started the Valium IV. It did not work.

Mom called the doctor back. He said to give Mike more of the Valium. She did that, but it still did not work.

The doctor told my parents that he could stop Mike's convulsion if we brought Mike into the hospital, because then he could put Mike under general anesthesia. Mom asked the doctor, "If you stop the seizure will Mike recover?"

The doctor said, "No, he'll die in a couple of days because it looks like he has CMV [cytomegalovirus] encephalitis and there's no cure for that."

Mom said, "We promised Mike that he could die at home, in his bedroom, surrounded by the people who love him. There must be something else you can prescribe that we can use at home."

The doctor told Mom that she could give him intravenous morphine, but the dose that he might need to stop the seizure might also stop his breathing.

Mom said, "You are telling me that he is going to die anyway. You are telling me that there is nothing left of his brain. The Mike that we know, the Mike who played video games and wanted to go to Disney World, is gone. The Mike who wanted to become a neurologist when he grew up is gone. If he goes into the hospital, he might live an extra day, but he will be unconscious and almost brain-dead.

"If Mike stays at home and I give him the morphine, he might die one day sooner because the morphine will stop his breathing. Mike does not want to die in the hospital. My husband and I do not want him to die in the hospital. Mike's brothers want to keep our promise to him.

"Mike can die at home. To let him live without thoughts, sights, and imagination is cruel. We're not so selfish that we will keep his body alive for an extra day or so."

Mom started the IV morphine drip. Mike's seizure finally stopped. It had been going on for ten hours!

Dad and Mom sat in Mike's bedroom with him. They told us to get some rest, but we wanted to be there when Mike died. So Adam, Erik, and I got out our sleeping bags and rested near Mike's bedroom door.

Mike's breathing sounded horrible. His fever went up to 109 degrees. Mike was deaf, and I always looked out for him when we were little and played outside. I was the brother who was most proficient at sign language. Now Mike needed help, but I couldn't help him.

I can't describe just how helpless I felt that night. I wanted my brother to live, but I wanted a healthy Mike. I knew that wasn't going to happen. So I prayed that he would stop breathing and die peacefully.

Suddenly at about one o'clock in the morning Mike stopped breathing. He had died—just eight hours before his flight was due to leave for Disney World.

I burst into tears. Dad hugged me. He was crying too. My brothers were crying.

I knew that Mike was no longer in pain. I believed that Mike was in heaven with our younger brother, Cubby. But I also knew how much I was going to miss him.

And I was mad, because Mike would never see his dreams come true. He would never become a neurologist. Instead he was dead.

As soon as Mike died, my parents called the doctor to come pronounce him dead. Then the saddest thing happened.

See, Mike had very severe hemophilia all of his life. Once when he was little, the doctors in the hospital had to stick his veins thirteen times. After that Mike made Mom promise that she would be the only one to put in his IV needles and take them out. So for years only Mom ever touched Mike's veins.

Usually, after Mom stuck us or took an IV needle out, she would kiss our arm. That night Mom said, "I cannot let the funeral director remove Mike's IV needle from his arm."

So, Mom gently took Mike's needle out. She kissed his arm for one last time and said, "Good-bye, Mike, my own Mickey Mouse. I love you."

Mike was fifteen when he died. He was my second brother to die of AIDS. I have AIDS. I don't want to die. I pray every day for a cure. In the meantime I take all kinds of medicines to keep me well. Some of these medicines are so toxic that they make me sick and nauseated all day long.

There was nothing my brothers and I could do to keep from getting AIDS, because we were born with hemophilia. We needed a blood product called factor VIII to help our blood to clot. We contracted HIV before we even knew that the virus was in the factor VIII.

Though there was nothing that Cubby, Mike, or I could have done to keep ourselves from getting AIDS, there's lots that you can do to avoid this disease. I wrote this to tell you that AIDS is a terrible disease. It is an ugly disease. There is nothing romantic or heroic about dying with AIDS. I know. I watched my two brothers die of AIDS.

CHAPTER 7

To the
Utmost of
Your Power

You do solemnly swear, each man by whatever he holds most sacred,
That you will be loyal to the profession of medicine and just
and generous to its members,
That you will lead your lives and practice your art in uprightness and honor,
That into whatsoever house you shall enter, it shall be for the good of the sick
to the utmost of your power, your holding yourselves
far aloof from wrong, from corruption,
from the tempting of others to vice,
That you will exercise your art solely for the cure of your patients, and will
give no drug, perform no operation, for a
criminal purpose, even if solicited, far less suggest it,
That whatsoever you shall see or hear of the lives of men which is nothing
to be spoken, you will keep inviolably secret,
These things do you swear. Let each man bow the head in sign of acquiescence.
And now if you will be true to this, your oath, may prosperity and good repute
be ever yours. The opposite, if you shall
prove yourselves forsworn.

HIPPOCRATIC OATH

THE MOST POTENT MEDICINE THAT RASPUTIN USED TO BATTLE THE
hemorrhages of the little czarevitch Alexis was trust. Alexis had
total trust in Rasputin. Traditionally, the link between healer and
patient is almost mystical. For thousands of years, tribal shamans
throughout the world have recognized that without faith in the

healer the patient would not be helped. In primitive societies the healers were also religious leaders, and when the shaman could not cure his patient's physical disease, his ministrations salved the troubled spirit.

Because hemophilia is a genetic disorder, affecting generation after generation in the same family, and because it requires specialized care from the cradle to the grave, hematologists come to know their patients better than most other specialists do. In many cases, physicians make friends of these patients. They commit their lives to assuaging their suffering and find that they cannot remain emotionally detached. The patients in turn become extraordinarily devoted to their hematologists. Even after relocating, patients often travel exceptional distances to maintain their association with a particular hemophilia treatment center.

With AIDS came loss of trust, destruction of long-term relationships, anger, and even hatred. Many HIV-infected people with hemophilia blame their physicians for their plight. Many of them are justified in feeling the way they do, and many are totally unreasonable.

Some patients believe their physicians knew that the clotting-factor concentrate they were prescribing in the early 1980s would cause them to develop AIDS. They also believe that these same physicians were financially motivated to continue prescribing contaminated clotting-factor concentrate despite the warnings being sounded in the medical community. Most think that because of the plasma-fractionating industry's generous research grants, the medical institutions to which their physicians were attached pressured these physicians to ignore the warning and continue prescribing the deadly product.

Many hemophiliacs insist that in order to avoid litigation, their physicians didn't share the truth with them. Litigation is a major reason for much of the anger that exists. When hemophiliacs filed suits against the manufacturers of their clotting-factor concentrates, hematologists came forward to testify for the defendants, the manufacturers. Many hemophiliacs believe that by testifying against them, the hematologists breached their trust. They even believe that some of the physicians who testified were motivated by the expert-witness fee, which could run to several thousand dollars.

Some members of the hemophilia community distrust their physicians because they think hematologists should have foreseen the devastating potential of a clotting factor that was not virally inactivated. They believe the medical community could have put pressure on manufacturers to develop a safer product.

Physicians, fearful of lawsuits and sensitive to the hostility surrounding them, have been reluctant to share their perspectives of this tragedy. Patients are rankled because their doctors have not said "I'm sorry." But doctors fear that such an act of simple human decency might be perceived as a legally binding admission of culpability.

The voices of the hemophilia community are not the only ones that need to be heard. The pain of the physician-treaters of the HIV-infected hemophiliac is real, and to deny it is to accept that these people were immoral ogres. They were not. They were ordinary human beings of whom too much might have been expected.

The humanity of their physicians is something patients have difficulty accepting. Physicians are held in awe because they save lives. Judaism, for instance, a religion of ancient origins that is deeply entrenched in tradition and law, vouchsafes the righteousness of the saving of human life. This is why Talmudic law allows hemophilic sons to be exempted from circumcision. Likewise, the laws of the Sabbath may be broken for the sake of preserving human life.

People who turn to a career of saving lives fulfill a special and honored role in society. But they are not omnipotent. They are not omniscient. They are certainly not prescient. "Our medical students are perhaps some of the finest young people in the nation," says the director of admissions at one of the country's most prestigious medical schools, "and their intellectual abilities are superior, and what they accomplish is awe inspiring. But the public tends to have unreasonable expectations of physicians." Science and medicine are specialized fields. You cannot expect a hematologist to take on the responsibilities of a retrovirologist no more than you can expect a cardiologist to perform brain surgery.

All of this must be taken into consideration by members of the hemophilia community when they ask, Why didn't the doctors know we were going to contract AIDS from our blood products? Why didn't my doctor tell me to stop using the factor? Why didn't my hematologist know how dirty this product was? Why didn't my hematologist do something about this? Why didn't my physician know this disease was going to kill?

Some physicians failed to ask the right questions. Others made incorrect deductions based on the available data. Some believed what they were told by the manufacturers of clotting-factor concentrates. Still others simply succumbed to peer pressure.

One prominent hematologist recalls a tour of Armour's Kankakee, Illinois, facility in the years before clotting factor was heat-treated. Her understanding was that Armour's paid plasma donors were college students. This physician trusted Armour because she had seen plasma-collection centers belonging to two of its competitors, Alpha and Cutter in the seedy Castro District of San Francisco, heavily populated by gay men, and in a rundown neighborhood in San Antonio, Texas.

In fact, Armour contracts with Plasma Alliance for its plasma supply. Plasma Alliance, a subsidiary of Rhône-Poulenc Rorer, which also owns Armour, currently does not, and never did, restrict its plasma collection to college students. "Many of Plasma Alliance's collection centers are located in college towns, but some are not," a company representative says. "Many college students donate plasma, but many donors are not college students."

In the wake of the sexual revolution, college students would not necessarily have guaranteed a safer clotting factor anyway. In a recent CDC study of college students who had been diagnosed with a sexually transmitted disease, 50 percent of them also tested positive for hepatitis B. Among college students with no history of sexually transmitted diseases, but a total lifetime history of more than three sexual partners, 14 percent tested positive for hepatitis B. Among college students with no history of sexually transmitted diseases and a lifetime history of fewer than three sexual partners, the rate of hepatitis B was 2 percent. When one considers the high correlation between hepatitis B and HIV, these figures are astounding–especially because many college campuses hold annual blood drives.

Nevertheless, the myth of Armour's collegiate plasma led the medical director of one hemophilia treatment center to order only Armour clotting-factor concentrates for the center–only to discover in late 1995 that Armour had been importing some of its plasma from Africa in the mid-1980s.

Myths and misperceptions about AIDS itself affected the decisions of many physicians. A hematologist recalls that "once testing was available for HIV antibodies and we saw how many patients tested positive, we didn't realize that so many would die. We thought that this virus was like hepatitis B, and the presence of antibodies indicated that the infection had run its course." This same hematologist also believed that a small minority of patients would die from HIV, but the majority would survive with mild, chronic disease or no significant ill effects at all, as was the case with those infected with HBV. She explained, "Our expectation was based on what we knew."

This doctor and others like her were partially correct in their original assessment of HIV. Information was presented at the Eleventh International AIDS Conference in the summer of 1996 indicating that some people had tested HIV-positive over several years without developing symptoms of immune depression. The reason for this was what *Time* magazine described as a "double dose of defective copies of the CKR-5 gene." The CKR-5 gene produces a chemokine, a special protein that enables HIV to enter human lymphocytes. One defective copy hinders entry, and two defective copies make entry impossible. As a result of this minor genetic abnormality, many long-term survivors will remain symptom free. Unfortunately, in the majority of HIV-positive hemophiliacs the virus progressed.

Dr. Ruth A. Seeler, the associate department chairman of pediatrics at the Michael Reese Hospital and director of the Pediatric Hemophilia Center in Chicago, believed that HIV would run a course similar to that of HBV. Dr. Seeler recalls that she and her colleagues "were never taught anything about retroviruses [the category into which HIV falls]. It wasn't until 1986 that we learned how unlike hepatitis B the retrovirus was, and then I was devastated." Dr. Seeler recalls a conference at which she and her colleagues realized what was going to happen to their patients. "We sat there stunned. We felt too sick to even go to dinner."

Many hematologists noticed an increase in hepatitis in the years between 1966 and 1981, when HIV infected the blood supply. Some attributed it to the use of the new clotting-factor concentrates, and some did not. Most hematologists, however, preferred to treat their patients with the factor concentrate despite the increase in hepatitis symptoms.

The choice of clotting-factor concentrate over cryoprecipitate was due to the concentrate's quantifiable dosage, reduced fluid volume, and fewer immediate adverse reactions, such as fever and allergies. In addition, clotting-factor concentrate was more easily transported. Also, it took less time to infuse—a distinct advantage when treating babies. Some physicians, like their patients, were given no options about treatment protocol. Concentrate was the only treatment available at their particular medical centers.

On the other hand, some physicians never made the transition from cryo to clotting-factor concentrate. They believed from the outset that pooled-plasma products presented too great a risk of viral infection. The majority of their patients avoided HIV infection. Dr. Oscar Ratnoff of Cleveland's University Hospitals was criticized by his colleagues as being "too hysterical" when he took this stance. But of forty-two patients he treated only with cryoprecipitate, all but one remained free of HIV. Of the one seroconversion (a patient who tested HIV-positive), there is the possibility that during a cross-country trip, when he was treated for a hemorrhage at another hospital's emergency room, he received concentrate.

Some hematologists never knew that clotting-factor concentrate was processed from pooled plasma collected from populations at high risk for infectious diseases. Some thought that the concentrate was processed from the pooled plasma of only hundreds of donors. Others were told by the manufacturers that the plasma came from paid healthy donor populations. Many physicians switched their patients from concentrate to cryo when the early cases of AIDS in hemophiliacs were reported, but as one doctor wrote to me, "By the time the physicians were alerted to the danger, most patients were already infected with the virus that caused AIDS." Some patients refused to make the transition from clotting-factor concentrate to cryo in spite of being warned by their hematologists. This was especially true of men who traveled for business.

Some doctors suspected as early as 1982 that many of their patients would develop AIDS, but others did not come to this realization until 1989 or later. Dr. Susan Travis, pediatric hematologist at the Cooper Hospital–University Medical Center in Camden, recognized early in the epidemic the danger that it posed to her patients, and she was horrified. She adjusted her treatment decisions accordingly, using cryoprecipitate whenever possible, especially with babies and young children. Like most of the other hematologists, however, Dr. Travis did not know that the U.S. manufacturers of clotting-factor concentrate could have virally inactivated their products before 1982.

According to a number of hematologists, in 1978 the U.S. manufacturers asked the hematologists what they most desired in a clotting-factor concentrate. They claim that they told them, "Get the viruses out!" The hemophilia community should be asking the manufacturers, Why didn't you respond to the request of our physicians? In 1994, the Institute of Medicine established a committee to investigate the transmission of HIV to thousands of blood-product recipients in the early 1980s. On July 12, 1995, the institute concluded that neither the physicians nor their patients were adequately informed of the risks by the industry and government regulatory agencies.

CHAPTER 8

While Rome Burned

EVEN WHILE THE NUMBER OF AIDS CASES IN THE HEMOPHILIA POPULA-
tion escalated, the blood-products industry was attempting to conserve its losses–not the losses in human life, but losses in profits.
Manufacturers were concerned about potential up-front capital outlay
and maintaining market share. A few years later, courtrooms across
the land were filled with litigants and documents showing that suppliers of blood products were not acting in their customers' interests.

In 1995, in *Gary W. Cross et al. v. Cutter Biological et al.*, attorneys
Thomas W. Mull and James A. Marchand, Jr., wrote in a memorandum to a court in Louisiana:

> In his affidavit, Dr. [Thomas] Drees, former C.E.O. of Alpha Ther-
> apeutics, states that the pharmaceutical companies conspired and
> acted together to implement delaying tactics which thereby cre-
> ated an unsafe standard of care within the industry. Additionally,
> the pharmaceutical companies formed a "task force" in an at-
> tempt to conceal the true facts of the efficacy of the CDC's recom-
> mended surrogate testing procedures. The goal of the "task force"
> was to refuse to implement a test proven to be effective in elimi-
> nating 90% of the HIV-contaminated donors.

Excerpts from documents, letters, corporate memos, minutes,
and transcripts submitted to the Institute of Medicine or demanded

and subpoenaed by plaintiffs in *Wadleigh v. Rhône-Poulenc Rorer et al.*, a 1993 federal class-action suit, and other hemophilia-HIV litigations reveal corporate subterfuge, crassness, and almost sociopathic amorality in the face of an unfolding human tragedy.

From a Cutter memo dated December 13, 1982:

> Donahue [Dennis Donohue of the FDA] specifically asked if we could simply exclude high-risk plasma taken from areas such as New York, San Francisco, and Hollywood from AHF [antihemophilic factor] production. Mike Rodell [CEO of Armour] responded that he felt a more meaningful effort would be to attempt to educate the high-risk populations (homosexuals, Haitians, and drug users) and have them voluntarily exclude themselves from the plasmapheresis programs.

From a Cutter memo dated December 21, 1982:

> Donahue [Dennis Donohue of the FDA] requested that we send him some official notification of our plans so that he could use this as ammunition that voluntary efforts of the industry precluded the need for any further regulation or activities in the FDA compliance area. He reiterated his concern that emotional media presentations such as last Friday's "Nightline" would only make our jobs more difficult and could result in further pressure from various sources. . . .

From a Cutter memo dated January 17, 1983:

> We also agreed that the CDC was getting increasingly involved in areas beyond their area of expertise and whenever possible we would try to deflect activity to the NIH/FDA. Apparently there were some major differences of opinion voiced at the ABRA [American Blood Resources Association] meeting last week between [Bruce] Evatt [of CDC] and Donahue [Donohue of the FDA]. . . .

The exclusion of high-risk donors would have significantly decreased the overall number of donors available to the manufacturers, and plasmapheresis centers in high-risk areas would have had to close. This would have been the only sure way to exclude high-risk donors, but it would have resulted in an immediate financial loss to the plasma fractionators.

Rodell's comment about a "more meaningful effort" to get high-risk donors out of the program leaves open the question of more meaningful to whom? Different high-risk groups had different reasons for choosing not to defer. For example, there should have been grave concern expressed regarding the ability of the IV drug abusers to rationally consider self-deferral. These particular donors, desperate for drug money, often went from one plasmapheresis center to another, donating their blood as frequently as possible and sometimes more frequently than was permitted. Expecting this population to voluntarily exclude itself from a blood-donation program that was its principal source of income would have been naïve.

During this period, power struggles were taking place among various public health service agencies. The FDA seemed overly concerned about the CDC overextending its authority. The CDC was more zealous about instituting stringent donor-screening and deferral procedures than was the FDA. There was also what some deemed an unhealthy cronyism between the FDA and the blood-banking industry. This relationship arose as a result of mutual blood-policy decision making. A majority of voting seats on the FDA's Blood Products Advisory Committee (BPAC) were held by people representing the industry.

Dennis Donohue was the director of the Division of Blood and Blood Products at the FDA's National Center for Drugs and Biologics. The tone of his approach to the industry, epitomized by his concern about *Nightline*'s emotional presentation, demonstrates an inappropriate solicitousness toward industry cronies and an indifference toward the people who might contract AIDS from blood products.

From a Cutter memo dated December 29, 1982:

> It appears to me to be advisable to include an AIDS warning in our
> literature for Factor IX and Factor VIII. I realize that very little is

known about AIDS and the relationship the products we manufacture have in causing the syndrome. However, litigation is inevitable and we must demonstrate diligence in passing along whatever we do know to the physicians who prescribe the product.

Whatever Cutter's motivation for advising doctors of the risk of transmitting AIDS via clotting-factor concentrate was, labeling the containers the factor came in would have clearly warned physicians and their patients. That these risks were not well understood by doctors or patients was evident at the October 1983 annual meeting of the National Hemophilia Foundation, where Dr. Margaret Hilgartner, medical director of New York Hospital–Cornell Medical Center's hemophilia center, presented an overview of the risks of contracting AIDS, indicating that the chance an individual riding a bicycle would be injured was one in fifty whereas the chance an individual receiving a blood transfusion would contract AIDS from that transfusion was one in one million. Patients report that from 1982 to 1984 their hematologists were telling them that clotting-factor concentrates were so highly processed that the causative agent of AIDS couldn't possibly survive in the concentrate. Others were being told that it just wasn't logical for companies to kill off their customers.

It should not be surprising that patients were not more alarmed by the reports of AIDS having been diagnosed in a handful of hemophiliacs, since by late 1982 only twenty-seven articles on AIDS had been published in major U.S. newspapers. So little media attention had been given the AIDS epidemic in the gay community that hemophiliacs had no idea of the implications of the disease. They were aware that a few people with hemophilia had died of AIDS, but they didn't understand how and why.

"I thought back then that getting AIDS meant that you were fine one day, sick the next, and dead on the third day," one hemophiliac admitted recently. "No worse than dying of a bleed in your brain. I didn't know that it meant months of suffering, becoming demented, or ending up a living skeleton lying in bed, wearing a diaper, with tubes running everywhere. AIDS just wasn't real to us. Nobody told us what it meant."

The recommendation to include a warning on concentrate labels was not acted on until 1984. By July 1984, the CDC's *Morbidity and Mortality Weekly Report* had documented the results of HIV antibody testing on a sample of asymptomatic persons with hemophilia A who were using clotting-factor concentrate: 72 percent tested positive.

From a Cutter memo dated January 4, 1983:

Primary concern was the possibility of a recommendation for further testing of plasma, particularly the anti-Hepatitis B Core Antibody (AntiHBC). Rodell (Armour) pointed out that this test would exclude approximately 10% of all potential donors based on a series of studies done at three of Hyland's [Baxter's] centers (6% positive in Duluth, 14% in Spokane and 12% in San Bernardino). . . .

From a Cutter memo dated January 6, 1983:

The two ever recurring proposals for actions to prevent AIDS in hemophiliacs seemed to be:

1. Conduct an educational campaign on the subject to all homosexual populations and allow them to voluntarily exclude themselves as blood and plasma donors. Gay Rights definitely in favor of first part, greatly opposed to lat[t]er.

2. Conduct anti-HBc [hepatitis B core antibody] testing of all blood and plasma donations—reject all "positive" from use in transfusable products. Question of cost and implementation bothered many but not CDC. . . .

From an American Red Cross memo dated February 5, 1983:

To the extent the industry (ARC/CCBC/AABB) [American Red Cross, Council of Community Blood Centers, American Association of Blood Banks] sticks together against CDC, it will appear to some segments of the public at least that we have a self-interest which is in conflict with the public interest, unless we can clearly demonstrate that CDC is wrong. A January 1983 incidence figure which is consistent with November and December 1982 and inconsistent with CDC's hypothesis of doubling every 6 months would be helpful in this regard.

CDC studies at that time demonstrated a nearly 90 percent correlation between an AIDS diagnosis and testing positive for the hepatitis B core antibody. One can only wonder what the motivation would have been, other than money, for not wanting to eliminate these donors. Testing became an issue of financial concern on two counts.

First, plasma fractionators considered plasma a raw material. In this particular industry, shortages of raw material result in smaller quantities of the finished product. The less the industry had to sell, the less it earned.

Second, according to an NHF report, the price of hepatitis B core antibody testing was five dollars. This amount would have increased the cost of producing clotting-factor concentrate by two and a half cents per international unit. According to this estimate, two thousand units of clotting factor–the approximate amount necessary to treat a knee-joint bleed in the average adult hemophiliac–would cost an additional fifty dollars to produce if the plasma of each donor were tested.

This money could easily have been recouped by passing the cost of testing on to the consumer. In 1983, the cost of factor VIII concentrate to the consumer was approximately twenty-five cents per unit. Today the cost of some brands of factor VIII concentrate runs well over a dollar per unit, ostensibly because of improved quality and safety. The price of clotting factor began to increase dramatically with viral inactivation. If the market was able to bear the increased cost of clotting-factor concentrate in 1986 or 1990, it would have been able to bear the increased cost of clotting-factor concentrate in 1983 or earlier. The hemophilia population is a captive market. One industry argument against surrogate testing–testing for hepatitis B core antibody as a marker for AIDS–was based on the effectiveness of the test, but one must question the sincerity of such an argument when a memo reveals that the "question of cost and implementation bothered many."

In May 1982, the total number of reported AIDS cases was 355. By November 1982, a total of 788 cases had been reported—more than double May's number. By February 1983, the total number of cases was 1,025, hardly an encouraging figure to use in an argument against surrogate testing.

By May 1, 1984, when the Irwin Memorial Blood Bank in San Francisco became the first blood bank to initiate surrogate testing, nearly 5,000 cases of AIDS had been reported in the United States. Irwin instituted its program because it had the highest rate of transfusion-transmitted AIDS of any blood bank in the country, and because experience showed that volunteer-donor deferral didn't work. Nevertheless, the American Red Cross still opposed surrogate testing and criticized Irwin's actions.

From a memo from Dr. G. M. Akin, director of medical services for Cutter, to Dale R. Dickinson, president of the National Hemophilia Foundation, February 15, 1983:

> No plasma collection centers which Cutter operates are located in any of the major "epidemic" cities such as New York, San Francisco, Los Angeles or Miami.

From *ECHO* (Education and Communication for Hemophiliacs and Others), May 1983:

> Cutter owns or contracts with over 80 plasma centers throughout the country. There are no Cutter centers in New York, San Francisco, Los Angeles or Miami, where the vast majority of AIDS cases to date have been reported.

From Dr. Akin to Dr. J. Lewis Manning of Volunteer General Hospital, Martin, Tennessee, September 16, 1983:

> I point out that we have no plasma collection centers in any of the five major cities where a high percentage of the AIDS cases have been reported. Most are located in small cities and towns throughout the U.S.

Despite Cutter's constant efforts to assure consumers that none of its plasma-collection centers was located in high-risk areas, its internal documents, submitted as evidence in court cases, demonstrate otherwise. A May 2, 1984, Cutter "Quality Assurance Document" lists plasma centers located in New York, Los Angeles, San Francisco, and other cities known to have the highest incidence rates of AIDS in the United States.

From a Cutter memo dated January 17, 1983:

> Curiously, Alpha inquired whether chimp studies would be required for approval of a heat-treated AHF product. Donahue [Dennis Donohue] indicated that they would probably approve the use of this procedure without chimp studies if the manufacturer could prove that it had no effect on the efficacy of the product. The message here is that Alpha is not very far along with their heat-treated product program. . . .

From a Cutter memo dated January 24, 1983:

> Jan Peterson spoke on the projected loss of Cutter AHF business expected if Hyland or other manufacturer is licensed for U.S. sale of a heat treated AHF prior to Cutter licensing. She encouraged the group to do everything possible to expedite our efforts toward having a licensed product available for sale.

From a Cutter memo dated May 24, 1983:

> On a short term we are facing a crisis. Our competitors have succeeded to come out first with a limited claim product. Forced by circumstances, the FDA granted approval without asking for solid evidence, as they asked Cutter two years ago. It is clear, that we have to fight the fire with a short term solution that will preserve our market position but not relent work and resources to be able to claim freedom from contamination by disease causing agents. . . .
>
> The problem of investments for a hepatitis-safe dedicated unit has been raised, and it was pointed out that dry pasteurization avoids this costly investment. In our opinion, a validated hepatitis-free unit for a hepatitis-free product cannot be avoided. As long as we do not claim a hepatitis-free product and neither the dry or wet pasteurization as we know them now do claim it, we do not have to invest in such a manufacturing facility.

From an Armour memo to its sales force, dated June 23, 1983:

For your information, the National Hemophilia Foundation issued a medical bulletin last month addressing the AIDS controversy and the use or non-use of antihemophilic concentrate by hemophiliacs. With the media coverage being given to the AIDS issue over the last few months, many hemophiliacs have discontinued or cut down on the usage of AHF concentrate for treatment during bleeding episodes.

The NHF in this bulletin is urging hemophiliacs to maintain the use of clotting factor in their treatment of hemorrhagic episodes as prescribed by their physician, emphasizing that the incidence of AIDS in hemophiliacs is very low and that life and health of hemophiliacs depends upon blood products.

With the position taken by the National Hemophilia Foundation, and many leading hematologists, with respect to the AIDS controversy the usage of antihemophilic concentrate is now moving toward pre-AIDS levels, a trend expected to continue in the next few months.

From a Cutter memo dated October 27, 1983:

I was impressed with the level of information presented by competitive manufacturers regarding their methods of manufacturing a heat-treated or viral inactivated concentrate. It is imperative for Cutter to remain in a leadership role to introduce product or products which demonstrate an increased degree of safety.

From the minutes of the October 15, 1985, meeting of the Recombinant DNA Steering Committee of Revlon Health Care (Armour), in Tuckahoe, New York:

Anita Bessler stressed the absolute need to duplicate the data of our competitors because we are in danger of losing a large part of our market share to our competitors. In her view, if we could establish that our heat treatment meets the claims of our competitors at least we could compete on the market while we continue to work to determine if, indeed, there is detectable virus at the lower cutoff. . . .

Bill Terry asked Mike [Rodell of Armour] whether we should approach the FDA with our preliminary results showing detectable levels of virus. . . . Rodell noted that it would be unwise to go to the FDA without completing our own work first. Mike pointed out that FDA has not conducted viral inactivation studies and the FDA has not required data on current market products so long as the manufacturer affirms the products are heat-treated. We have the least heat-treated product and we're trying to get FDA approval for our product, so we must provide the data. In Mike's view, the issue is not one of regulation, but rather marketing.

Mike Rodell noted that if we did increase our heating to 68 degrees, 72 hours . . . we would need new pharmacological and toxicity data vis a vis safety for the FDA . . . if we modify our heat treatment process at Kankakee we're going to incur potentially major expenses. Our competitors had to "retool" their facilities in order to go to the higher temperatures. So there's tremendous corporate exposure here and we're losing markets everywhere each month that there's a delay.

The 1986 plans for production of AHF is at 60 degrees and 30 hours. A change in the temperature requirements would require an enormous amount of work just to take care of our current product lines. Anita Bessler re-emphasized that changes in heat treatment at the Kankakee plant could cost in the range of $6 to $20 million.

There can be no question that industry competition was the primary motive for the development of safe, effective virally inactivated clotting-factor concentrates. It is important to remember, however, that when representatives of the plasma-fractionating industry attended the very first Public Health Service meeting in July 1982 to address the issue of AIDS diagnosis in hemophiliacs, they knew that viral inactivation was needed. They also knew that a process that could achieve that not only existed but was available to them. Behringwerke had published information on its process the preceding year. But rather than pay for another company's patent and agree to market another company's product, the plasma fractionators engaged in a race to win market share by developing their own virally inactivated product. And preparing to race takes time.

How acceptable is the disingenuousness of a company that would lead consumers to believe its product was virally inactivated, while admitting in a corporate memo that "As long as we do not claim a hepatitis-free product . . . we do not have to invest in such a manufacturing facility"? Dry-heat treatment at sixty degrees Celsius for thirty hours versus heat treatment in solution at sixty degrees Celsius for ten hours meant little to consumers. The majority of patients knew that heat treatment meant killing the viruses. They didn't realize that only some of the viruses were being killed, and not all methods were equal.

While companies were developing their own viral-inactivation processes, consumers contracted HIV. Even after some virally inactivated products were brought to the market, consumers still contracted HIV. Armour worried about what it would cost to adapt its facility to a new process. The six million to twenty million dollars it would cost to make changes to the Kankakee plant may seem exorbitant, but was it really such a high price to pay when in one year the cost of factor VIII for my family alone was nearly one million dollars (covered mostly by insurance and/or Medicaid)? Armour did not withdraw its inadequately heat-treated product from the market until December 10, 1987, when six Canadian patients using the product tested HIV-positive. The FDA denies that it was informed of the presence of HIV in the Armour product in 1985, but then "in Mike's view, the issue is not one of regulation, but rather marketing."

When the Commission of Inquiry on the Blood System in Canada received a copy of documents from Armour relating to the issues discussed in the October 15, 1985, meeting, pages and pages of information were blacked out. The portion of the minutes that appear here was considered by Armour to be some of the less damaging evidence. One can only imagine what secrets lie under the blacked-out portions of the documents.

From the argument presented before the U.S. Court of Appeals for the Seventh Circuit in Chicago by Douglas Fuson, attorney for Armour, on behalf of all four manufacturers of clotting factor, January 30, 1995:

> It's important here to consider that these matters involving blood products are near and dear to the public-policy interests of individual states as reflected in the blood statutes that have been enacted to protect the supply of blood and blood products for people who require them—whether they be persons with hemophilia or people who simply need blood transfusions.

While Douglas Fuson addressed the court about how a series of state statutes known as blood-shield laws had been enacted to protect the blood supply, I grew restless. I knew Fuson was speaking with a forked tongue. Those laws were enacted to protect the processors and providers of blood products, not the consumers.

I looked over at little Roger, my friend Dee's grandchild. Roger, a hemophiliac with AIDS, was eleven years old, the age of my Cubby when he died. And I thought more about Mike. Roger was dying of progressive neurological deterioration, an effect of AIDS. His brain was just shriveling up in his sweet, fuzzy-haired head. Watching Roger that day was especially painful to me because he was using the reclining wheelchair that had belonged to Mike and Cubby. Because Roger resembled Mike physically, I suffered from flashbacks all afternoon.

Roger could no longer sit up unsupported. He hadn't been able to walk for more than a year. His eyes were misfocused. He couldn't smile or frown because his face was so pathetically paralyzed. His little fingers were painfully hyperextended. He wanted a drink of water, but he couldn't ask for it. All that he could do was make a loud moaning sound.

Roger came to Chicago that day in January 1995 for the hearing on decertification of the federal class-action suit, *Wadleigh v. Rhône-*

Poulenc, Rorer et al., which had been filed by members of the hemophilia community at about the same time Roger became paralyzed. Dee, on Roger's behalf, was one of the representative plaintiffs.

I thought of a picture I have at home showing a grinning Roger in a baseball cap. He's holding a fish aloft. It's one that he caught himself. Roger loved to fish. Now all he could do was lie down and moan. He couldn't feed himself or play with toys.

I was especially infuriated as I listened to Douglas Fuson so sadly misrepresent the blood-shield laws. They certainly didn't protect the blood products that Mike, Cubby, and Roger used, though Roger's case was different from my sons' cases. Mike and Cubby were infected by a product that was not virally inactivated. Roger, born two years after Cubby, had the supposed advantage of using a virally inactivated product.

Unknown to Dee but as the manufacturers should have anticipated, given the scientific findings discussed at their October 15, 1985, meeting, Roger's blood product, Armour's Factorate, was contaminated with HIV. Roger had used a product that was unsafe because its manufacturer was in a hurry to get its own product to consumers cheaply and not lose market share. The manufacturer could have used Behringwerke's process of heat treatment in solution or another one, but that would have added too much inconvenience and expense to the manufacturing process. So Dee infused Roger with an unsafe product.

The product that Roger used was recalled by the FDA on December 10, 1987–and only then through the initiative of the Canadian government–but by that time Dee had infused Roger not one time but twenty-seven times with four different lots of it.

Roger's loud moans were starting to disturb the courtroom, and Dee stood up to take him outside. As she wheeled Roger by, I thought morbidly, "Soon that wheelchair will have outlived its three little owners."

The morning of June 21, 1995, I wanted to sleep late. I hadn't been able to fall asleep the night before. Cubby died in June 1993, and since then June has been a tough month for me. It's the month that I must make arrangements for the Cubby DePrince Memorial Award—a plaque and fifty-dollar bond given by our family each year to a graduating sixth-grader from the Richard Stockton Elementary School in Cherry Hill.

It was the second graduation day since Cubby died, and I still couldn't trust myself to make the presentation personally. I cried just thinking about it, so my friend and Cubby's, Sally O'Brien, the school nurse, would present the award in my place.

I forced myself to wake up and face the day. I had work ahead of me. I had changes to make in my manuscript for this book. I had to rewrite a pamphlet for the Hemophilia Association of New Jersey.

While Teddy was eating his breakfast, I listened to the morning's messages on my answering machine. The first message was from Dee: "Elaine, please call me." I could tell by the sound of her voice, because I'd heard that stunned, strained tone from too many friends already, that Roger had died in the night.

I returned Dee's call. She shared her relief—Roger would no longer suffer. She shared her sorrow—she would miss him desperately. She shared her anger—he shouldn't have died. "I want to press criminal charges," she said. "I think Armour knew that clotting factor was contaminated. Do you think that I can prove it? Do you think I have grounds for criminal charges?"

In order to answer Dee, I broke a confidence. I had made a promise that I would tell no one that I possessed copies of both the Prince Report and the Meloy Report, two documents intended as evidence in the federal class-action suit. These reports, along with many other documents from the files of the manufacturers of clotting-factor concentrate, had been sealed by an order of the court. (Since Roger's death, they have been made available by the Commission of Inquiry on the Blood System in Canada.) Contraband copies of the reports had been floating around, and from them I learned the truth about the clotting factor that killed Roger.

I told Dee the truth that morning because I didn't believe any court had the right to keep any portion of the truth about this disaster from its victims. "Dee, Armour was dry-heat-treating its product at sixty degrees Celsius for thirty hours. The company suspected that the temperature was too low to kill viruses using the dry-heat treatment. It brought a sample of the product to a New York scientist. He tested it and found live virus. The Prince Report is his report."

Armour sought a second opinion from its own lab. The second opinion was the Meloy Report, and it corroborated the findings decribed in the Prince Report.

Dee asked, "What did Armour do with the product after they learned that it contained live virus?"

I explain that the company left it on the market for two years and eventually sold it to Canada. Six Canadians contracted HIV from it. Five of them were children. The Canadians have since filed suit in Philadelphia and settled for $1.5 million.

Dee gasped at these facts. "They murdered Roger. I want to get them. Not just in a civil suit. Money isn't going to bring Roger back to me. I want them punished. I want criminal charges brought."

One month before what would have been his twelfth birthday, Roger's body was weighed and measured for his casket. He was five feet one inch tall. He weighed thirty pounds.

The report made by the Institute of Medicine of the Academy of Sciences in 1995 concluded:

> In the Committee's judgement, heat-treatment processes to prevent the transmission of hepatitis could have been developed before 1980, an advance that would have prevented many cases of AIDS in individuals with hemophilia. . . .

In a reference to decisions that were made regarding donor screening and surrogate testing in the early 1980s, the institute concluded:

> The FDA made several decisions in 1983 that appear to have been influenced by the blood-industry-based [profit and nonprofit] members of the BPAC [Blood Products Advisory Committee]. The FDA . . . allowed statements and recommendations of the BPAC to go unchallenged. . . .

The prominence of representatives from blood banks and blood-product manufacturers on the Blood Products Advisory Committee, with no balancing influence from consumers and no process within the FDA to evaluate its recommendations, is a failure of advisory committee management. Perhaps advisory committees should contain fewer topical experts and more members with expertise in principles of good decision making and the evaluation of evidence. A committee so constituted might run a reduced risk of standing accused of having conflicts of interest.

The fact that the same companies who wrote self-serving communications regarding clotting-factor concentrate also served on the FDA's Blood Products Advisory Committee sends a chilling message about unethical priorities and serious conflicts of interest. To date, no criminal charges have been brought against the manufacturers of clotting-factor concentrates, though residents of more than one state are advocating this.

CHAPTER 9

The Blood-Shield Laws

If a man has stolen a child, he shall be put to death.
If a builder has built a house for a man and has not made his work sound,
and the house he built has fallen and caused the death of its owner,
that builder shall be put to death.

CODE OF HAMMURABI

HUNDREDS OF LAWSUITS WERE FILED BY MEMBERS OF THE HEMOPHILIA community in attempts to establish that the manufacturers of clotting factor are liable for the transmission of HIV to hemophiliacs. The courts more often than not upheld the defense attorneys' arguments that since hemophiliacs contracted HIV before the availability of a test for antibodies, the manufacturers of clotting factor could not be held liable.

But then on June 4, 1996, the New Jersey Supreme Court made a precedent-setting ruling in what will inevitably become a landmark case. In a six-to-one decision, the court said that the American Association of Blood Banks was negligent in the case of William Snyder, who received a transfusion of HIV-contaminated blood during open-heart surgery in 1984. Justice Stewart Pollock ruled that the AABB could have screened donors more stringently, and he suggested that it neglected to institute hepatitis B core antibody (surrogate) testing because of "the added inconvenience and costs that the test would have required."

Before *Snyder v. AABB,* courts weighed the claim of risk versus benefit. "The blood-banking industry claims that transfusion equals a resuscitation measure," Bruce Evatt of the CDC explained. "Without the transfusions, the patients would have died anyway." But this was not the case with clotting factor, which was frequently used for routine, non-life-threatening bleeds.

One way for hemophiliacs to plead their case is for them to point out that given the many dubious plasma sources and the large donor pools, not to have virally inactivated the blood products against hepatitis B was unconscionable and negligent. Yet this plea has not been successful because the National Hemophilia Foundation touted factor VIII concentrate as the standard of treatment for patients with severe hemophilia A throughout the first half decade of the AIDS epidemic. Doctors all over the country treated their patients with this product. Studies published in reputable medical journals approved the use of the clotting factor despite its viral contamination. Even the co-director of the National Hemophilia Foundation argued against viral inactivation as late as December 1982.

Charles has volunteered to drive our motor home on a circuitous tour of the Midwest. It's late June 1994, hot and muggy. Sprawled on the sofa behind us, Teddy complains that a trip to Ohio, Michigan, and Illinois is not his idea of a fun vacation.

I tell him not to complain. We could be making this trip in a car and sleeping in a tent at night, as we did years ago. At least we'll sleep in comfort.

As we drive along, I am often overwhelmed by melancholy. We used the motor home primarily for the two-hundred-mile round-trip to the children's clinic in Newark and secondarily and more joyfully for vacations. Inside the clean, climate-controlled behemoth, I would run IV drips into children who were sick enough to be hospitalized but, thanks to our family's willingness and their physicians' cooperation, could live normal lives. Normal for us, that is. Few families would consider running intravenous medication in Shenandoah National Park normal.

On this particular trip, Ted is hooked up for a six-hour drip of intravenous gamma globulin. He dislikes this monthly procedure and grouses sardonically, "It's actually fun, compared to being lost outside of Detroit in bumper-to-bumper traffic. I get to watch the gamma globulin drip into the chamber. That's a lot more exciting than watching the cars not move on this giant parking lot of a highway." I ignore Teddy. He's at that age—thirteen years old, with three months until he starts high school.

We manage to find a campground in the Detroit area, and I visit a hemophilia-HIV family that evening. The following morning we are headed to Illinois, where I've made arrangements to meet the Smith family.

Fred and Lisa live in a modest but beautifully cared for home on an average-looking street in the average-looking town of Edwardsville, Illinois. They have two children: Brent, a bright, quiet twelve-year-old boy, and Cassie, a vivacious eight-year-old girl. As I listen to Lisa speak, I realize that despite Fred's hemophilia, for years this family lived a typical American heartland life. Fred went to college. He had a job as a systems analyst. Lisa worked part-time when the children were little. She moved on to a full-time job as they grew up.

The family worked on their house, doing the painting, papering, paneling, and woodworking. Fred and Lisa were interested in their children's schoolwork and attended Little League games. The refrigerator was always covered with school papers, homemade Mother's Day and Father's Day cards, and car-pool schedules. It still is, but for the most part the present of the Smith family differs radically from the past.

In the early 1980s, Fred contracted HIV from his factor VIII concentrate. Fred believes he has much to be thankful for. He and Lisa started their family without even knowing of the potential threat of Fred's HIV. Lisa could have contracted HIV from Fred, and the children could have been born with it.

As I look at Fred, I marvel that he can still find something to feel thankful for even though he is skeletal and appears to be totally drained of energy. Fred is a gentle soul, serene and courageous. With great spiritual strength he is preparing for the death he will soon face.

Lisa is trying to match Fred's courage and serenity, but there is a certain fragility to her composure. I can tell that one wrong word from me will open up the floodgates that now contain her fury and despair.

When Fred is out of the room, Lisa tells me that she sometimes feels overwhelmed. All of the normal responsibilities of family life fall on her shoulders, and in addition she cares for a dying husband. "I doubt that we'll ever celebrate another wedding anniversary," she says. "I want to spend as much time with Fred as possible, yet I worry. With no medical benefits, what will I do if one of the children gets sick? Who will pay the doctor's bill? With what? If I pay the doctor's bill, how do we buy food?"

In addition to confronting the loss of her husband, Lisa must figure out how to maintain a reasonable standard of living after Fred's death. "You know how impossible it's always been for a hemophiliac to get a decent life insurance policy," she explains. "So we hoped that we could get compensation from the companies. We filed suit, and we lost. That was the summer of 1991."

Fred has returned from a laborious walk to the bathroom. "It wasn't as though they questioned the source of my infection," he tells me. "My doctor knew I was heterosexual. I'm not an IV drug user. We're monogamous. We just couldn't prove that the companies were negligent."

As Fred tires, his voice softens. I can barely hear him, so Lisa takes over the telling of their appalling tale. "You know, they brought in the big guns for their defense. Some of these guys were on MASAC [the National Hemophilia Foundation's Medical and Scientific Advisory Council] in the eighties. Can you imagine? They give us such rotten advice then, and now they testify against us. One even had the nerve to say that he had no reason to believe that HIV-positive hemophiliacs would go on to develop full-blown AIDS! How could he say something like that in 1991!

"Of course, we lost the case. Now we can't sue again. I think we sued too early. I think that we should have waited. I think more evidence will come out to prove us right and them wrong."

When I leave after lunch, I know that I will never again see Fred alive.

In late 1992, the National Hemophilia Foundation requested that "any health professional currently serving on the Medical and Scientific Advisory Council or the Board of the National Hemophilia Foundation not accept any responsibility in testifying as an expert witness in a way that might impair persons with hemophilia from pursuing legal remedy against manufacturers of clotting factor concentrates in courts of law." But this resolution does not affect those who previously served on the council, so in fact several prominent hematologists who advised hemophiliacs to continue to use clotting factor when it was in fact dangerous are now serving as experts in cases that question their actions.

That the defense counted heavily on the testimony of the big guns is evident in this letter from attorneys for Cutter Laboratories to a lawyer who was representing HIV-infected hemophiliacs from Costa Rica in 1985:

> Cutter is most saddened by the report of the unfortunate demise of your clients who apparently contracted AIDS through the use of AHF that you contend was manufactured and supplied by Cutter Laboratories.... Certainly, we sympathize with the families of these unfortunate individuals. It is my assumption that the individuals were hemophiliacs who benefited greatly, throughout their entire lives, from the product manufactured by Cutter (and others) which allowed these unfortunate hemophiliacs to live as close to a normal life as possible.
>
> The AHF manufactured by Cutter was done so in strict compliance with all of the requests, guidelines and demands of the National Hemophilia Foundation, which looks after the interests of hemophiliacs in this country. Cutter was at the forefront of at-

tempting to deal with this dreadful situation in a manner that was responsible and compassionate. Should litigation ensue, I am certain that you will find that the leading hematologists in this country will be acting as experts on behalf of Cutter Laboratories. In fact, should litigation be commenced in your area, the current Medical Director of the National Hemophilia Foundation will act as an expert witness on behalf of Cutter.

Please understand that, absent some truly unusual situation, there will not be, and cannot be, any settlement of your cases.

Once most of the big guns were prohibited by the National Hemophilia Association from testifying in defense of the manufacturers, HIV-infected hemophiliacs faced two remaining foes: statutes of limitation and blood-shield laws. Blood-shield laws exempt blood products from strict product liability.

Strict product liability is a legal concept that permits a purchaser, consumer, bystander, or any other person who is injured by a defective product to file suit against the manufacturer, wholesaler, distributor, or seller of a product. Once damage is done by a defective product, the manufacturer, wholesaler, distributor, or seller of the product is liable for the harm, whether or not negligence exists on any or all parts.

The clothes one wears, the automobile one drives, the deodorant one uses, the aspirin one takes for a headache, and the toys one's children play with are all subject to strict product liability. Yet the blood that is dripped into a person's veins is exempt by statute from strict product liability in forty-seven of the fifty states. Someone who has been injured as a result of a transfusion of any type of blood product can hold the manufacturer of the blood product liable only if he or she can prove that the manufacturer failed to exercise "due care" in the preparation, manufacture, writing of instructions, labeling, or some other part of the process by which the product is prepared and delivered to the consumer. Since there is no objective standard for measuring due care, the outcome in such a case relies heavily on the interpretation of individual judges and juries. Because the state of Illinois has a blood-shield law, Fred Smith lost his

case. He was unable to prove negligence on the part of the companies that manufactured the blood products he received.

Blood-shield laws have come into existence in the United States in
two different ways: as statutory law and as case law. In forty-seven
states, the blood-shield laws were introduced by bills passed in state
senates and state assemblies, and are therefore statutory laws. In
the District of Columbia, a blood-shield law was established as the
result of a court decision and is therefore case law. Because case law
is determined by the precedents set in court hearings of similar
cases, it is more open to interpretation than statutory law. In statutory law, however, the issue of legislative intent is taken into consideration when a case appears before the court.

The legislative intent of the blood-shield laws is particularly difficult to establish, since few states have maintained records or transcripts of testimony dating back to the 1960s or 1970s, when most
blood-shield laws were enacted. New Hampshire is an exception,
and transcripts of testimony on its blood-shield bill given in committee in the early 1970s are enlightening. The records clearly indicate an effort to protect blood banks, doctors, and hospitals. That
House Bill 203 (HB203) was heard before the state Judiciary Committee and not the Health and Human Services Committee is a sig-
nal that it was meant to deal with lawsuits, not with health care
issues.

A lobbyist opposed to the bill testified that its basic purpose was,
"to provide by statute that the doctrines of strict liability and
breach of warranty shall not apply in cases of blood transfusions
and tissue transplants. . . . In a breach of warranty, a person who
sells a product gives a warranty including a warranty that it is fit
for the use for which it was intended." By exempting blood products from "breach of warranty," this bill would in effect exempt the
seller of the blood (the blood bank, plasma fractionator, manufacturer, and so on) from providing a product "fit for the use for which
it was intended."

When State Senator Robert English asked whether there was to be
"any provision to tell the patient that there is danger," another lob-

byist, this one from the American Association of Blood Banks, which supported the bill, replied, "The law requires that you get the patient's consent. In recent years, there is a doctrine growing that the patient is supposed to be reasonably informed by the doctor before giving his consent."

According to the transcript, no one at the hearing remarked that the AABB lobbyist did not answer Senator English's question. The senator wanted to know whether or not the patient was to be informed that the blood transfusion presented a risk to his or her health. But English did not pursue the line of questioning.

A blood bank director testified that "the chief danger is in blood purchased from professional donors. No such blood is used in New Hampshire and Vermont." It is probable that this blood bank director, from a small hospital in New Hampshire, had not handled, and therefore had adequate cause to forget, the clotting-factor concentrates. Whether failure to consider hemophilia patients using paid-donor clotting factor was deliberate or accidental cannot be determined at this point, but the upshot was that a blood-shield law that was represented to the New Hampshire state senators as a means of protecting doctors and small hospitals in a rural, sparsely populated state resulted in protecting multibillion-dollar corporations.

During the committee hearing, a lobbyist for the New Hampshire Medical Society appeared to be representing the financial interests of patients when he said that "hospital costs might be substantially higher due to increased insurance rates for malpractice. In Illinois, it has been estimated that [the settlement in a case in which a patient contracted hepatitis from a transfusion] would add about $20 a day to a room of a 400-bed hospital."

The plaintiff in Illinois was Frances Cunningham, who died before a decision was rendered in her case. Her beneficiaries received a settlement of $50,000 from MacNeal Memorial Hospital in Berwyn, Illinois. Even if this money was not paid by the defendant's insurance, it was certainly not enough to radically increase the cost of a hospital room. An increase of $20 a day in the cost of a room in even a small 100-bed hospital would raise the hospital's income by almost $750,000 in one year, which would allow for a $50,000 settlement with almost $700,000 to spare. Yet the statements by the New Hampshire Medical Society lobbyists went unchallenged.

According to another lobbyist supporting the blood-shield law, "Court action would cut down the motivation to donate." But there was no question of blood donors being sued. No laws existed to prevent hepatitis carriers from attempting to donate blood. Yet this lobbyist's statement, too, went unchallenged. The only effect that a lawsuit could feasibly have on blood donation is to force the blood-banking industry to exercise greater diligence in selecting donors.

In the New Hampshire Judiciary Committee meeting, all interested parties were represented except one. No one testified on behalf of the patients. The New England Hemophilia Association was conspicuously absent, as was the American Cancer Society, the Leukemia Society of America, and other organizations that were involved with patients who regularly receive blood products.

It is possible that consumer-interest groups were unaware of the existence of this bill. Few citizens realize that they are entitled to receive by mail, upon request and free of charge, a copy of the legislative calendar for their state; a citizen can simply telephone his or her state's legislative offices and subscribe to the calendar. All the sessions of the state's senate and assembly are listed, including committee hearings, as are the bills that will be heard. Anyone can testify at a committee hearing. One need only appear a few minutes before the hearing begins and register with a committee aide who is present in the hearing room. Legislators are not experts on the multitude of issues presented before them for a vote. They must rely on the guidance of informed testimony. This is why special interest groups hire lobbyists. Such groups also guarantee the attention of their legislators by making campaign donations. Since small nonprofit organizations lack the funds of megacorporations, it is not surprising that bills that benefit corporations and harm individual citizens often win legislative votes.

In the 1996 presidential campaign, the ten leading contributors to both parties' nominating conventions included two major pharmaceutical companies—Abbott Laboratories and Baxter International. Abbott was the early manufacturer of Profilate, a clotting-factor concentrate whose license was transferred to Alpha in 1978. Baxter has been in the plasma-fractionating business for several decades and is still involved in the manufacturing of clotting-factor concentrate.

———————

June 6, 1994. Elena Bostick asks me whether I can be in Trenton by 9:00 A.M. She wants someone from the Patient Services Committee of the Hemophilia Association of New Jersey to testify before the New Jersey State Senate Health Committee. Since doing anything for the hemophilia community helps assuage some of my rage and grief, I agree to be there.

I am supposed to address an amendment to an insurance bill. The amendment will require insurers who offer bare-bones insurance policies to provide the same coverage for blood products used at home as they provide for blood products used in the hospital.

Elena has provided me with a copy of a statement. It looks stilted to me. If I memorize it, I'll sound like a first-grader in a play or a robot. I ask whether I can just put the statement in my own words. Elena agrees, so I give it some thought while testimony on other bills is being heard.

Finally it's my turn. Pete McDonough, a former New Jersey state senator and world-class swimmer, as well as a dear friend to the New Jersey hemophilia community, accompanies me to the front of the room. I sit at a huge conference table and begin my testimony.

At first, I freeze; then words seem to come unbidden to my lips. I feel as though I were watching myself on a television screen.

I explain to the senators that "Hemophiliacs require the infusion of clotting factor, a blood product, to prevent or stop the hemorrhages associated with their disorder. This blood product can be administered either in a medical setting, such as a doctor's office or emergency room, or it can be administered at home.

"What does this mean to the insurance company? Administration in a medical setting requires that the insurance pay for more than just

the cost of the blood product. For example, if it is administered in an emergency room the insurance company must pay the emergency room fee, the physician's fee, and the cost of the blood product. If it is administered at home, the insurance company need pay only for the blood product itself.

"What does this mean for the patient? The sooner a hemorrhage is treated, the less likely it is that permanent damage will occur. . . . This past summer my son Erik was babysitting for a neighbor's children. Suddenly the elastic cord on one of their toys broke and snapped across Erik's eyes. Within fifteen minutes, Erik, with the help of his younger brother, had been able to infuse himself with his blood product. When we arrived at Philadelphia's Wills Eye Hospital after an hour of struggling through rush-hour traffic, we were told that the accident had lacerated Erik's corneas and precipitated bleeding into the anterior chamber of his eye. The physician who examined him said, 'He has some vision loss, but it will be temporary. If Erik had not been able to stop his bleeding by treating [himself] with his clotting factor, he would probably have been blinded permanently.'

"Erik is a talented cartoonist. He will earn his living with his hands and eyes. Without the immediate administration of his blood product in the home, he would be blind, and he might have needed to rely on taxpayers' dollars for support."

As I complete what I think to be clear and eloquent testimony, State Senator John Matheusen says, "I have a question, and perhaps it's only me, but I know that your organization has testified before our committee in the past. . . . My colleagues may already understand this, but I don't. What is this treatment for hemophilia? What does this entail?"

From the embarrassed expressions on the faces of some senators, I realize that few if any of them understand what treatment for hemophilia involves. Yet they have heard testimony on hemophilia-related issues in the past and have voted on hemophilia-related bills. I wonder what would motivate a group of lawmakers to vote on an issue without understanding it. So I explain the simple procedure of administering clotting factor to oneself.

I notice that the senators look surprised and a little perplexed. I suspect by the expressions on their faces that they thought some highly technical medical expertise was needed for the administration of this treatment. Finally a senator blurts out, "Is that all!" There are murmurs from the others. One senator asks, "Is there any opposition to this bill? If not, let's vote on this. It certainly makes sense." The opposition, unable to argue with common sense, backs down.

As I leave the building, I reflect upon the amount of bad legislation that has passed. This is not surprising, but what I do find surprising is that often bad legislation is passed even without campaign contributions or special efforts from lobbyists. Bad legislation is sometimes passed because no one was there to speak out against it.

Due to a lack of opposing testimony, some inaccurate and propitious testimony, and ill-informed legislators, New Hampshire became the twenty-sixth state to enact a blood-shield law. From 1971 to 1976, the blood-banking industry hustled blood-shield laws through the legislatures of twenty-two states. Eight additional states passed blood-shield laws either during or in the wake of the transfusion-acquired AIDS epidemic. In North Dakota and several other states, the paragraph on legislative intent says that the statute was passed in order to protect the medical and scientific community from lawsuits.

Some of the same states that passed blood-shield laws, making it almost impossible for patients to be compensated for transfusion-related damages, had previously passed laws that contributed to the contamination of the blood supply. Legislation passed in Arizona, for instance, allowed the sale of plasma from the state prison. Even though prisons are notorious for their high hepatitis rates, the manufacturers of clotting-factor concentrate used prisons as plasma farms. Six years after the Arizona legislature approved the harvesting of plasma and whole blood in its prison population, it passed a blood-shield law excluding blood from strict product liability.

The danger of hepatitis transmission in plasma, especially pooled plasma, was well recognized by the medical community in 1945, yet with the exception of California, states did not begin passing blood-shield laws until the mid- to late 1960s. It is neither unreasonable nor illogical to suspect that the sudden appearance of these blood-shield statutes was motivated by the industry's knowledge that the new clotting-factor concentrates were responsible for hepatitis transmission rates of nearly 100 percent. The timing of the blood-shield laws was synchronous with the marketing of clotting-factor concentrate.

The timing of California's blood-shield law is curious, however. It was passed in 1955, a full decade before any other state introduced similar legislation. "The only effect that this bill would possibly have, so far as we are aware, is with respect to the sales and use tax," a lawyer for the state wrote at the time, although this was questioned by a deputy attorney general who sent Governor Goodwin Knight a very curious interdepartmental communication speculating that the legislative intent was something different from what it appeared to be, especially since human blood and plasma had been exempt from a sales tax in California since 1946. The statute was placed in the Health and Safety Code, which meant it could be used to exempt from strict product liability "whole blood, plasma, blood products and blood derivatives for the purpose of injecting or transfusing the same into the human body."

Since all other states that passed statutory blood-shield laws did so following the clinical trials of clotting-factor concentrate, it has been a mystery why California had a blood-shield law so much earlier on. I think the key lies in a small vial on a shelf in Cleveland, Ohio. Dr. Oscar Ratnoff pointed it out to me. It contains Cohn Fraction I. Developed by Dr. Edwin Cohn in the 1940s and manufactured in California by Cutter in the 1950s, Cohn Fraction I is a blood product—a plasma fraction that contains fibrinogen, other concentrated clotting factors, lots of virus, and other impurities. It is manufactured from pooled plasma. "It was used primarily to treat women who hemorrhaged in childbirth," Dr. Ratnoff explained. "It was filthy. Every mother who received it contracted hepatitis, and often so did her baby. I would never use it. I've kept it all these years to demonstrate to my students the danger of these pooled plasma products."

Weeks later, back in my office, a telephone call to the FDA yielded no information about Cohn Fraction I, other than the fact that it was never licensed. "Did Cutter ever apply for a license?" I asked a representative of the FDA's Center for Biologics Evaluation and Research. Information concerning products that do not gain approval is not public information, I learned from her. I also learned the astonishing fact that the FDA doesn't have a record of all products made from human blood or plasma that are developed. The FDA representative told me that if a product is developed and used within a state's boundaries and is not transported across state lines, FDA approval isn't required. A telephone call to Cutter in California, which is now a part of the Bayer corporation, yielded no better results. Neither its medical/technical departments nor customer relations could find any information about, or reference to, a product named Cohn Fraction I.

I feel that some blood-product-related secret lies buried in California, possibly along with a few patients. I wonder what besides Cohn Fraction I was being used in California that carried a tremendous risk for hepatitis. Something had to have been happening to motivate the passage of such an early blood-shield law. I learned that in 1964, Dr. Edward Shanbrom was invited by Hyland to become involved full-time in developing a clotting-factor concentrate for patients with hemophilia. According to Dr. Shanbrom, Hyland had been working on this concentrate for ten years previous to his arrival.

So two of the facilities involved in the development of clotting-factor concentrates in the 1950s were located in California. And California passed a cleverly disguised blood-shield law in 1955. It is difficult to believe that this was purely coincidental.

Even if the passage of blood-shield laws was totally independent of the development of any high-risk product, the result was that manufacturers of plasma-fractionation products could make choices based on profit rather than people. The same blood-shield

laws that reduced motivation to provide a safe clotting-factor concentrate now prevent hemophiliacs with HIV from winning their
cases. Yet ironically, these laws do not prevent the manufacturers of
clotting-factor concentrate from suing and winning large settlements from plasma-collection centers that "sold" them contaminated plasma.

---

*My friend Karen lost her hemophilic son, Brad, to AIDS. He had used
Cutter's clotting factor, which was manufactured from the contaminated plasma of donor X. Karen's daughter, Jen, is suffering the post-
trauma stress of having watched her brother slowly wither away.*

*Brad's story is particularly horrendous. He developed enceph-
alopathy years before he died. His behavior regressed from that of a
teenager to that of a small child. He became unpredictable and had
to be watched over. Eventually Brad's motor skills deteriorated. Finally he was blind, paralyzed, unable to speak.*

*Karen paces across my hotel room as she tells this story. We are in
Dallas at the annual meeting of the National Hemophilia Foundation. Seeing my teenage son Teddy living with hemophilia and AIDS
has dredged up unbearably sorrowful memories for Karen.*

*Karen begins to tell me about the emotionally exhausting ordeal of
the trial in her lawsuit against the manufacturers of Brad's contaminated clotting factor. "Our case is in appeal, Elaine. This will drag on
for maybe two or three more years. Until it ends, I can't lay Brad to
rest. What makes me so mad is that Cutter sued a plasma-collection
center in Texas. Some of the plasma that the Texas center supplied
was collected from a donor who later died of AIDS. Cutter collected
a multimillion-dollar settlement."*

*I jump up, shocked by what Karen has just told me. "How did you
hear about this?"*

*"It came out as evidence in Brad's trial. Nobody at Cutter had to die
for that money. But the blood-shield laws are preventing hemophiliacs from collecting settlements. I look at those guys downstairs [other
hemophiliacs with AIDS]; I look at your Teddy. It breaks my heart.
This is so wrong."*

I am numbed by what Karen has told me. After she leaves, I find that I cannot fall asleep. I think of the forty-something blood-shield laws that I have read through. It becomes a riddle in my brain. When is blood a service and not a sale? When is blood a sale and not a service? Why would a multibillion-dollar industry win a settlement but not Karen's son and my sons—and the sons of all the other mothers?

———————

Blood-shield laws served as a deterrent to the timely development and implementation of the viral inactivation of clotting-factor concentrate. An effective viral-inactivation process for bagged plasma has already been developed. Viral-inactivation processes for cellular-blood products are on the not-too-distant horizon. The question remains as to how the blood-banking industry will respond to their availability. Adopting them will add inconvenience and cost to blood-banking operations. With neither financial nor legal incentive, time alone will tell whether moral rectitude will provide the industry with adequate motivation.

CHAPTER 10

Loss and Compensation

THE FIRST THREE CASES OF AIDS IN HEMOPHILIACS WERE REPORTED in the Centers for Disease Control's *Morbidity and Mortality Weekly Report* in July 1982. In the first five years of the epidemic, an estimated ten thousand to twelve thousand hemophiliacs were infected with HIV. They die at the rate of one individual per day.

Hemophiliacs are, as a group, intelligent and well-informed. They work hard for what they want, legislatively and medically. Perhaps it's because of the years of childhood immobilization or life's harsher lessons learned too early, but whatever the reason, these are people who, with few exceptions, do not waste their lives. The hemophilia community has an exceptionally high rate of achievers: scientists, accountants, engineers, artists, musicians, chess masters, writers, lawyers, entrepreneurs, and so on.

Hemophiliacs form a communal bond with one another that supersedes racial, religious, and ethnic boundaries. They work hard to take care of themselves and their own. They rarely allow the public to notice their pain—physical or emotional. But AIDS is stripping them of these characteristics. Many hemophiliacs with AIDS now lack the energy to compete in the workplace, and some are too sick to work at all.

In all but a handful of states, insurance legislation is inadequate to meet the needs of unemployed hemophiliacs. These people, so used to making their own way in life, are suddenly finding themselves without employment and without insurance–because they have AIDS. Funds that were squirreled away for their children's education, their own retirement, or the purchase of a home are in many cases being used to pay exorbitant medical bills.

The National Health Care Financing Administration classifies hemophilia as the most catastrophic illness of any in terms of cost. Clotting-factor-concentrate costs run as high as $1.34 per international unit. A 150-pound adult with hemophilia A requires approximately 3,400 international units of clotting factor for a critical bleed. When the cost of AIDS is added to the cost of clotting factor, an uninsured hemophiliac's savings can dwindle to nothing in a matter of days.

As destructive as the financial loss from AIDS is to the hemophilia community, it is not the most significant loss. AIDS has increased the physical pain and suffering of people who were already burdened by more than their share of pain, and the emotional pain is immeasurable.

"I was born on January 2, 1962," Bryan Rilott tells me. It's now December 1993, and he's a thirty-two-year-old hemophiliac with AIDS. "My younger brother and I were both born with severe hemophilia A. The hemophilia prevented me from playing in sports, but having a brother and a friend with hemophilia normalized my life.

"I attended Northern Illinois University in De Kalb and graduated magna cum laude with a BS in computer science and applied data processing. I managed to complete the requirements for two minors, one in mathematical sciences and the other in business administration.

"Getting a job was no problem. Within days, I was employed by a large aerospace company as an applications programmer. I had planned to continue on for my MBA, but I couldn't resist the lure of such a good job. Besides, it was my lifelong dream to own a Corvette. With a good job, I could make that dream come true.

"I married Kathy fourteen months later, right after she graduated from nursing school. By 1990, I was sure I had the world by the tail.

We had two beautiful healthy little boys, Bryan II and Adam. I was in terrific shape. I was even able to reduce the number of joint bleeds I had by working out five days a week and weight lifting. Neither Kathy nor I smoke, and we don't drink.

"We bought a home in the suburbs because Kathy worked part-time as a nurse. She only worked on weekends, so I could take care of Bryan II and Adam. I liked spending the time with them. By then, I had been promoted many times. My salary was nearly double my original pay.

"In the spring of 1990, I developed a cold and a cough. In June 1990, I was diagnosed with PCP and AIDS. My T-4 count was only one hundred. I was started on AZT and was told I had only one year to live. The only good news was that Kathy, Bryan II, and Adam tested negative for HIV.

"A year later I developed wasting syndrome. I'm six feet two inches. My weight dropped from two hundred pounds to one hundred twenty pounds. I had to abandon my career in May of 1992. I publicly disclosed the cause of my illness because I wanted to provide AIDS awareness to those around me. Also I wanted them to know how hemophiliacs were infected by HIV through their clotting-factor concentrates. I wrote a message to all of the employees to that effect."

It is easy to recognize from Bryan's almost manic conversation that he doesn't believe he's got long to live. When he pauses for a breath, I ask him, "What is the hardest thing for you to deal with?"

"I know that some of these losses are going to seem insignificant, but—I miss my Corvette. When I was in college, I had this poster of a Corvette hanging in my apartment, and it said, ONE OF THE ADVANTAGES OF HIGHER EDUCATION. Once I couldn't work, I found it hard to rationalize the car payments, so I traded it in for something less expensive.

"Also, my weight loss bothers me. I can't ride my motorcycle. I don't have the bulk and the strength. For a kid who owned his first motorcycle in high school, it was painful to part with a Kawasaki 1100. It was part of my image—not so much to others, but to myself.

"I fell in love with this German shepherd puppy. I bought it and realized that it was unfair to keep it. I knew that as my physical condition worsens, the care of the dog is going to fall on Kathy's shoulders, and she has enough to deal with. It was too painful for me to part with the puppy, so while I was on vacation with Kathy and the boys, I telephoned my parents and asked them to do it. I told them to find a good home for it. I had named it Taz after the Tasmanian Devil, my favorite cartoon character.

"The loss of friends is painful. I had to weed out my friends. I was always too emotionally drained and too physically exhausted to give as much of myself as I need to maintain these friendships. I have to conserve most of my energy for Kathy and the boys.

"Ahh, my boys—I spend as much time with them as humanly possible. My boys give me the motivation to live. I want to teach them to bat and pitch, shoot baskets, and throw a football. I tell them, 'You're brothers. You should always be there for each other, like your uncle and your dad.'

"Sometimes I worry that my sons will forget me. They won't remember the good times we had or what my face looks like.

"I worry about Kathy. She's emotional, yet she holds everything in. I don't want things to be hard for her. I'm taking care of all the funeral arrangements. I went out and purchased plots. I chose the monument. It gives me peace of mind to know that Kathy won't have to do it."

I ask Bryan, "Are you in a lot of physical pain?"

"About the pain of AIDS—I have my good and bad days. Not a day goes by without some type of pain. I try not to let my wife and kids know about the pain. They have enough to deal with."

I ask Bryan, "Are you afraid of dying?"

"I worry, Elaine, that I'm going to die and that's going to be it. There won't be anything after this life on earth. That's not what I've been raised with, but the thought crosses my mind and terrifies me. Do you think that there's life after death?"

I set a date to visit Bryan and Kathy, but a month before my scheduled visit, Bryan died—bravely, but unnecessarily.

Newlyweds planning to have children postponed their plans when HIV arrived on the scene. Now many hemophiliacs have long passed the asymptomatic period of the disease. Couples have run out of time. Young husbands even less fortunate than Bryan are dying without leaving a part of them behind. Young brides have become young widows without having had the opportunity to become young mothers. Even hemophilic teenagers, anticipating their first date, are denied the normal coming-of-age rituals.

Returning from the kitchen with a cup of hot coffee, I pass Teddy's bedroom at the top of the stairs just before I turn right toward my office. Teddy is moping, grim faced, as he stares out the window, geometry book propped on his lap, paper crumpled by his bare toes.

"Ted, what's wrong?" I ask.

"Nothing," he mutters.

I perch on his bed, carefully balancing my cup of coffee. "Hey, Ted, you look so tragic." Teddy forces a tiny but bleak smile. He picks up the crumpled sheet of paper from the bed and silently hands it to me. I open it and press it flat with my hands.

Dear Teddy,

The reason I'm writing this is because we have been talking to each other through a lot of people lately and I think that I should start being honest with you. I guess the best place to start is at the beginning. When I first met you I really liked you. It was the first time I had ever met a guy with great looks and a great personality. But I thought there was no possible way you would ever like me.

I guess it was about a year later when I saw you again at Lindsay's party. I was so happy to see you. The next day people kept coming up to me and saying that you liked me. I was so excited. Then everyone was saying that you were going to ask me out. It was too good to be true. But, that's when I remembered a time that you and your mom came to my Hebrew school to talk about AIDS.

I understand the fact that you can't get it from kissing, because it takes 3 gallons of saliva, but what happens if both people have cuts in their mouths? I almost always have cuts in my mouth, because I wear a retainer at night and it cuts up my mouth. So, to be honest with you, I'm scared to kiss you because of AIDS. I will understand if you think that I'm acting really stupid, because I hate myself for being scared. If you don't mind, I really want to talk to you. Please tell me if you think I'm being ridiculous; I'd rather know than have you keep it to yourself. I'm so sorry I'm acting this way....

Teddy's eyes are filling with tears. He hates to be caught crying. I give him a kiss on the top of his head—not exactly an even exchange for a girlfriend's kisses. I have no words of comfort to offer him.

A wife, infected with HIV by her husband even before learning of his diagnosis, sometimes dies before him. Too frequently the first sign of the husband's infection is the diagnosis of AIDS in a newborn child. HIV-infected couples blessed with healthy children must face the prospect of leaving their children orphaned.

Mothers who once coped so well with their sons' hemophilia, maintaining their graciousness and sense of humor, have become hollow eyed and thin lipped with bitterness and anger. Hemophilia is a hereditary disease. Many of these mothers have lost more than one hemophilic child to AIDS. Empty-arms syndrome prevails among these women, as does guilt.

A mother's guilt springs not only from the inheritance pattern of hemophilia but also from the administration of clotting factor in the home. Certainly more than one mother has asked herself which infusion infected her son. Could he have managed with fewer infusions? Did she treat him too often? Should she have insisted on a different brand of clotting factor? Maybe his bleeds weren't so bad. Maybe he could have done without the clotting factor. Maybe she could have taken him to the hospital for cryo or fresh-frozen plasma and thus reduced his risk of infection.

Maybe . . . maybe . . . maybe . . . All these pointless maybes come from wonderful mothers, exemplary mothers, who feel they've somehow failed their children.

———————

Dee needs someone to talk to. She is feeling guilty. "My mother says that she didn't carry the gene for hemophilia. I'm the first person in the family to be a carrier. She says that I must have done something wrong to be a carrier. She says that I should have never given Roger the factor VIII that wasn't adequately heat-treated. She says that I'm a nurse. I should've known better."

"Oh, Dee," I answer. "You're beating yourself up. You know that we all feel guilty, but it wasn't our fault. Why are you doing this to yourself? For that matter, why do I do it to myself? Besides, you know where your mother's coming from on this."

"Yes, I know. She hurts, so she takes it out on me. She needs to take her anger out on somebody, and I guess I'm the closest."

———————

The fathers are often hardworking men who accepted jobs that offered the best insurance, not the greatest satisfaction. Many fathers held second and third jobs in order to make ends meet. They rejected employment opportunities because the promotions would mean a transfer to an area without adequate hemophilia care. Most of these fathers admit that they regret the time they couldn't spend with their sons because they needed to work too many hours to meet medical expenses. They torture themselves by fretting over past reprimands, groundings, punishments, no matter how well deserved.

———————

My husband, Charles, is following me. We reach the top of the stairs, and I turn left toward our bedroom. Charles turns right. He opens the door of Cubby's bedroom.

"What are you doing?"

"I'm sorry," Charles answers. Tears fill his eyes. "For a minute there, I forgot. I was going to tuck Cubby into bed. Where I really forget is in the supermarket. I find myself going down the aisle to pick up Mike's favorite cereal or those little microwavable hamburgers that Cubby used to love. It's like my mind just slips into an old memory pattern. Then I'm pulled sharply into reality, and it hurts."

————————

Uninfected siblings are angry, confused, guilty, and lonely. They've lost not only a sibling but, in many cases, their parents–the parents they used to know, the parents who could solve any problem.

————————

I am visiting Adam and have taken him to a nice restaurant for dinner. He's a doctoral student in computer architecture, and he can't afford nice restaurants, so this is a treat for him. As he tells me about some idea he's developing for a dissertation topic, he suddenly stops and gazes wistfully out the window.

"Mom, sometimes when I'm working at my computer, I think of Mike," he says. "Remember how he loved computers? He'd program his hard drive to crash just as his teacher typed in the word Algebra *or* Math. *Do you remember how he'd stand and look over my shoulder when I programmed? Then he'd try it on his own.*

"Sometimes when I do something that's particularly brilliant, I think, 'This one's for you, Mike.' "

————————

Family events that should abound with joy become poignant reminders of the loss. A young man's wedding day is overcast by the shadow of the missing brother who would have been his best man. A young woman with a baby looks for the features of her brother in the newborn's face, hoping that something of her brother survived–some genetic trait.

For all these losses, the hemophilia community deserves compensation. Not just because hemophiliacs developed AIDS–other people developed AIDS, and they aren't demanding compensation. The hemophilia community is demanding compensation and deserves compensation because it is the only community to become infected through the use of an FDA-approved product. Both industry and government failed it.

The United States is one of the few industrialized countries that has failed either to legislate or facilitate the process of compensation to its hemophiliacs infected with HIV. People diagnosed with AIDS receive a modest Social Security income and disability payments, but this is small compensation for a young man who has spent twenty-three years in school to obtain a PhD, only to become too debilitated by AIDS to earn a living. There are also strings attached. A father with hemophilia can't save money for his child's education without risking the loss of his benefits. For young men wanting to prove their independence, wanting to be productive, these strings became a stone wall. The meager income maintenance under the Social Security system is accessible only when the patient's resources are almost completely depleted.

Such a system of maintenance cannot be considered compensation for a disease acquired by the use of a government-regulated product. The programs available to hemophiliacs with AIDS have not been modified to address their unique circumstances. The industry that caused the transmission of HIV to the hemophilia population is not involved in the provision of benefits or compensation. Essentially nothing has been done to provide compensation.

In some cases, the manufacturers of clotting-factor concentrate who refuse to compensate hemophiliacs in the United States have participated in the compensation of citizens of other countries, such as Germany, Japan, Sweden, and Switzerland. Where the manufacturers have failed to provide compensation, governments took up the slack. Government compensation in other countries has run as high as $475,000 per person, often without requiring that the patient waive his right to a lawsuit.

Most of the countries that have provided compensation to HIV-infected hemophiliacs and their families have national health care programs, and the payments were intended either to maintain the infected or affected individual's standard of living due to loss of income or compensate for pain and suffering. Sweden specifically announced that payment to HIV-infected hemophiliacs who are asymptomatic is considered compensation for deprivation of sexual relationships.

Since the United States has no national health care program and state laws exempt manufacturers of blood products from strict product liability, our efforts at providing compensation are more in line with those of nonindustrialized countries. South Africa, Jamaica, Brazil, Greece, and Uruguay have not provided compensation to hemophiliacs with HIV either. India, Malta, and Malaysia, on the other hand, have either strict liability laws or damages-to-health legislation. It is possible for hemophiliacs in those countries to collect compensation through the courts on the basis of the damage that has been done to them regardless of the negligence of the clotting-factor manufacturers.

Repeatedly the four major manufacturers of clotting-factor concentrate in the United States made it clear in meetings and by letter that they did not wish to become involved in the compensation of hemophiliacs with HIV. They steadfastly maintained that they were not at fault for the epidemic of blood-product-acquired AIDS among U.S. hemophiliacs. Two of the corporations involved in the Japanese settlement were Bayer Yakuhin, Bayer's Japanese subsidiary, and Alpha's parent company, Green Cross. The U.S. subsidiaries of these parent companies delayed taking action when dealing with hemophiliacs.

When offers were finally made to settle the class-action lawsuit of hemophiliacs in the United States, the settlements were subject to Medicaid and Medicare subrogation, were inadequate, or were ridden with unacceptable provisos. The issue of subrogation is serious because the cost of treating hemophilia and AIDS is high. When a patient is required to repay Medicaid from his compensation, the compensation could disappear into the government's coffers, and the victim might not see a penny.

As for the provisos, many people in the hemophilia community viewed strings-attached settlement offers as a corporate effort to separate victims with a good case from those with a weaker case or a case filed after the statute of limitations had run out. One ploy has been to include an opt-out clause when offering small settlements. With such a proviso, if more than a stipulated number of claimants choose not to accept the settlement, the offer is rescinded.

Hemophiliacs who live in a state without a blood-shield law and have filed lawsuits within the time allowed by their state's statute of limitations on product liability often stand a chance of winning in court. They would be foolhardy to settle for a small, out-of-court class-action settlement when they can win a larger settlement in court. But they feel pressure from the thousands of hemophiliacs who live in states with blood-shield laws and are outside their state's statute of limitations. Many with apparently hopeless cases are in desperate financial straits. A great deal of bitterness has built up within this usually close community because of the conflicting needs of the two groups of HIV-infected hemophiliacs.

One mother says, "My son is dying. He's seventeen years old. All I want is enough money to buy him a new car. That's all I need to bring a little happiness into his life. I'll agree to a one-hundred-thousand-dollar class-action settlement."

Another mother says, "I've lost my only child to AIDS. When I grow old, who will be there for me? I won't have a son. I won't have grandchildren. The cruel fact of life is I'll have to pay someone to take me to the supermarket and care for me if I break a bone. I'll be helpless and lonely. One hundred thousand dollars won't even pay for the help to replace my son and the nonexistent grandchildren, let alone compensate me for the grief and loneliness."

———

On August 7, 1994, the Honorable John F. Grady of the U.S. Circuit Court, Northern District of Illinois, certified a class-action suit filed by hemophiliacs against the manufacturers of clotting-factor concentrate and the National Hemophilia Foundation. The hope that Grady gave hemophiliacs was short-lived, however. The case was decertified on March 16, 1995, by Chief Judge Richard A. Posner of the Seventh Federal Circuit Court of Appeals. In one fell swoop, twelve years after the first U.S. hemophiliac was diagnosed with AIDS, Judge Posner denied thousands of HIV-infected members of the hemophilia community and their families the right to a class-action suit.

Posner's decision focused on the economic hardships that a class-action suit would impose on the manufacturers. He expressed concern that a class action would force "these defendants to stake their companies on the outcome of a single jury trial, or be forced by fear of the risk of bankruptcy to settle even if they have no legal liability." Posner also pointed out that "a notable feature of this case . . . is the demonstrated great likelihood that the plaintiff's claims, despite their human appeal, lack legal merit. This is the inference from the defendant's having won 92.3 percent of the cases to have gone to judgment."

Judge Posner based his statistics on thirteen cases, the majority of which were heard before the plaintiffs had accumulated much of the incriminating evidence that was gathered by the team of class-action attorneys during discovery. He also did not take into consideration that each of the previous cases had been fought in isolation by financially restricted plaintiffs represented at times by financially restricted law firms, who faced Goliath-like companies with huge bankrolls with which to finance their defense.

Hemophiliacs are investigating other solutions to the problem of lack of compensation. The Ricky Ray Hemophilia Relief Act of 1995, which was supported by 249 federal legislators, authorized one billion dollars to be used to compensate HIV-infected hemophiliacs, infected spouses, and children and beneficiaries. It was not as generous as the Canadian, Australian, French, or Japanese compensation packages, but it was better than nothing, which was what hemophiliacs with AIDS in this country had heretofore received. Nevertheless, the bill was doomed, not least because its language cast blame on governmental agencies for failing to adequately regulate the blood-banking and plasma-fractionating industries.

Neither the concept of compensation nor the amount being requested by the hemophilia-HIV population was presumptuous or unprecedented. Similar compensation has been made to other groups, in some cases when the government was not even partially responsible for the damages, as it was in the hemophilia-HIV epidemic. Private industry has been required to provide benefits to victims of black lung disease, radiation exposure, swine-flu vaccine injury, and childhood vaccine injuries.

"I think the American system is not very good. . . . It would be a lot better if we could establish a trust fund for all victims," said Dr. Thomas Zuck, professor of transfusion medicine at the University of Cincinnati Medical Center's Hoxworth Blood Center, in testimony before the Commission of Inquiry on the Blood System in Canada in the spring of 1995. Dr. Zuck is a blood bank director who, as a past president of the American Association of Blood Banks, had previously testified in behalf of blood-product manufacturers. But he has modified his position and now recommends a no-fault system that would allot equal compensation to all HIV-infected victims of blood products. "At least that way we could get the medical care, the family care, and a reasonable amount so that they could have some kind of life with dignity," he said.

In addition to compensation, hemophiliacs in the United States need closure. Some entity must accept responsibility and apologize. In Japan, executives of corporations that produced and marketed contaminated clotting factor in the 1980s bowed down, heads to the floor, begging forgiveness of Japanese hemophiliacs and their families. This was *dogeza,* a form of apology that in Japan is second only to ritual suicide in its gravity. The hemophiliacs of the United States are asking simply for fair compensation and an apology.

CHAPTER 11

Risks and Regulation

IT TAKES TEDDY JUST MINUTES TO RECONSTITUTE HIS FACTOR VIII AND infuse it. On most school mornings, this is usually the last thing he does before he dashes out the door. He doesn't suffer hives, asthma attacks, headaches, or fevers as a consequence of the infusion. And he feels confident that it will not make him sick–a grave concern to him, because he contracted chronic hepatitis B, chronic hepatitis C, and HIV from earlier factor VIII products.

Clotting-factor concentrate has come a long way since it contaminated thousands of hemophiliacs with hepatitis and HIV over a decade ago. Today it is available in three levels of purity: intermediate, high, and ultrapure. Teddy uses an ultrapure genetically engineered (recombinant) factor VIII that is produced in hamster ovary and kidney cells, not in the cells of human beings. The latest genetically engineered clotting factors are freeing hemophiliacs completely from dependence on human-donor plasma.

Genetic engineering is the key to the development of recombinant factor VIII. One glitch in the new process, however, is that the recombinant factor is suspended in human albumin, which, because of laboratory errors in processing and testing, offers the remote but still possible risk of viral contamination. But even more advanced recombinant products have been developed that do not use human albumin. Their efficacy and safety will ultimately lead to the complete abandonment of clotting-factor products made from human blood—with all the inherent problems of donor screening, blood labeling, testing, and viral inactivation.

The recombinant factors licensed in the early 1990s made the treatment of hemophilia nearly risk free, but that is not the case with other blood products. Bagged plasma used in trauma units, packed red blood cells used in surgery or to treat certain diseases, and other bagged blood components still carry a risk of infection.

The rate of transfusion-related HIV plummeted after screening of donor blood for the virus began in 1985. Today the American Red Cross tells us that the risk of becoming infected with HIV from a blood transfusion is 1 in 400,000. The National Institutes of Health tells us that the risk is 1 in 250,000. The figure used by the NIH is calculated by extrapolating from the number of cases of HIV infection in the general population, but the problem with this is that no one knows how many people in the United States are infected with HIV. Doctors are required to report cases of AIDS but not cases of HIV infection. According to guidelines established by the Centers for Disease Control, AIDS can be diagnosed if a person over thirteen years of age has a T-4 lymphocyte count of less than 200. But by the time the T-4 count of someone infected with HIV falls to 200, he has harbored the virus for anywhere from one to fifteen or more years. During that period, he might not have been aware of his HIV infection, and he could have unintentionally transmitted the disease to others sexually, or by sharing dirty needles or syringes, or by donating blood. His contacts would in turn have transmitted the virus to other contacts.

As much as three weeks to forty-two months could pass between the time a person was infected with HIV and the time the infection showed up in standard tests. (In 95 percent of cases, this "window period" is over within six months of infection.) In 1995, the FDA recommended (but did not require) that blood-collection centers use an HIV p24 antigen test to screen donor blood. The difference between this test and an HIV antibody test is that the HIV p24 antigen test will sometimes detect HIV during the window period of infection. It doesn't always do so, however. Even people with AIDS who have harbored HIV for years can test negative for p24 antigen.

Contaminated blood can also slip through a net of safety procedures due to human error: instructions on test kits and equipment are not followed; critical steps are missed, and blood is thus incompletely tested; mistakes are made in recording data or labeling samples. Cracked bottles caused a deadly bacterial contamination of one company's plasma products in 1996. Defective computer software used by more than two hundred hospital blood banks was recalled in 1995 when the FDA discovered that programming defects could lead to the release of contaminated blood.

As far as the risk of contracting HIV from contaminated blood products goes, the guesstimate of 650,000 to 900,000 cases of HIV infection in the United States is not a very satisfactory point from which to extrapolate the odds. Dr. Bruce Evatt of the CDC says that "the best way to determine the risk is to conduct follow-up studies of transfusion recipients." Such studies show us a startlingly different risk rate from those offered by the American Red Cross and the NIH. Follow-up studies of heart surgery patients indicate HIV infection rates of 2 in 11,500. Studies of other transfusion recipients indicate a rate of 1 in 60,000. This is negligible in comparison with the 1 in 3,300 risk of transmitting hepatitis C through a blood transfusion, which persists despite the introduction of hepatitis C screening of donor blood in 1989. Such a rate is horrifying if one takes into account that hepatitis C is not a one-shot deal. For the majority of patients, hepatitis C is chronic and lifelong. Chronic hepatitis C infections lead to 80 percent of liver transplants.

The quality of the screening for hepatitis C has been affected by cost-cutting measures. Until 1995, blood was screened for ALT (alanine aminotransferase), a liver enzyme that is elevated in the blood if a patient's liver is irritated, inflamed, or infected. An ALT test is not a specific test for a specific disease but, rather, a general test for liver function. Eliminating prospective blood donors with elevated ALT levels eliminates donors who are in the infectious window period for hepatitis B and hepatitis C, as well as donors with hepatitis E, hepatitis G, and hepatitis H–viral infections that are either uncommon in the United States or so new that screening for them is not yet in place. But when hepatitis C screening tests were improved, the FDA discontinued the ALT test. This saved the blood-banking industry millions of dollars each year. It also enabled it to use thousands of units of donor blood that would have been discarded in the past–blood of questionable quality.

Patients are sometimes not aware that they are being treated with a blood product and that there might be some risk involved. Blood products do not always come in a bag hung from an IV pole. A person with a rusty nail in his foot will receive a tetanus immune globulin injection in the emergency room if his tetanus boosters are not up-to-date. Someone bitten by a strange dog will receive a rabies immune globulin injection. An Rh-negative mother who has just given birth to an Rh-positive child will be injected with Rho D immune globulin. Patients born with a primary immune deficiency, lupus patients, AIDS patients, and others receive intravenous gamma globulin.

For years it was believed that immune globulins contained too many antibodies to transmit active disease, and for years intravenous products manufactured from immune globulins were not virally inactivated. Then when it became clear that some patients had contracted hepatitis C from intravenous gamma globulin, manufacturers recalled implicated lots and began virally inactivating their products in much the way clotting-factor concentrates are treated. In January 1992, the FDA recommended that all plasma-derived products be virally inactivated, and followed this recommendation with a reminder in May 1994. Yet injectable immune globulin products are still manufactured without being virally inactivated. In fact, even products that have tested positive for hepatitis C can be used. On March 14, 1995, the FDA sent health practitioners a letter advising them that when products that test negative through polymerase chain reaction (PCR) tests for the hepatitis C virus are unavailable, "practitioners should be advised to continue to use first untested, then PCR-positive intramuscular immune globulins with an appropriate discussion with patients of the risks and benefits." Since the patients who use the injectable immune globulin products are usually not chronically ill but are receiving prophylactic treatment to avert something like rabies or tetanus, it is doubtful that any of these "healthy" patients ever receive follow-up screening for hepatitis C infection.

Only the most common blood-borne viruses are screened in the United States: HIV-1 and HIV-2, hepatitis B, hepatitis C, and HTLV I and II. To test for all blood-borne viruses would be impossible. Reliable and convenient tests just do not exist for all these viruses. Yet the list of blood-borne pathogens is intimidating. It includes human herpesvirus-6, Epstein-Barr virus, cytomegalovirus, B-19 human parvovirus, the alphabet soup of hepatitises, and a newly recognized strain of HIV that eludes current donor blood screening tests.

It is easy to imagine a scenario in which an exotic virus—one of the many that are not screened for—invades the nation's blood supply. Something like Lassa fever, for instance, which can be blood borne and has a seven- to fifteen-day incubation period. Its appearance in this country is far too rare to warrant blood screening. Consider, though, this hypothetical situation: A traveler who has been infected with Lassa fever returns to the United States totally unaware of his infection. He has no symptoms for two weeks, and during this time he donates blood. His plasma goes into a pool that provides a product to hundreds of people. Since Lassa can also be transmitted by inhaling viral particles, the hundreds of people infected by the plasma product could then infect a multitude of others.

Another rare disease that could be transmitted in a transfusion and that is not vulnerable to currently used methods of viral inactivation is Creutzfeldt-Jakob disease (CJD), which became a household word in 1996 when it was linked to "mad-cow disease." CJD is believed to be caused by a prion, a small proteinlike infectious particle, although some virologists think that a yet undiscovered virus will eventually be implicated as the cause. Prions are now the "best bet," however, because they are implicated in the transmission of certain other "slow" viral diseases–diseases with incubation periods of ten to thirty years. Prions cause certain human diseases, such as kuru, which occurs among a cannibalistic tribe in New Guinea. They are also the cause of sheep scrapie and a form of brain disease seen in mink.

There have been documented CJD transmissions via corneal and dura mater (lining of the brain) transplants, tympanic membrane (eardrum) grafts, and injections of human pituitary growth hormone, but until 1995 there were no documented cases of CJD linked to blood products. Then a fifty-seven-year-old woman died of CJD two years after having a liver transplant. According to an abstract presented at the seventy-first annual meeting of the American Association of Neuropathologists in San Antonio, Texas, "the liver donor had no history of neurological disease. A small proportion of albumin transfused during and after the transplant came from a patient who died 3 years later from a dementia with clinical and EEG features suggestive of CJD."

Dementia is a hallmark of CJD, and though most up-to-date textbooks on infectious diseases recommend that blood donations from patients exhibiting symptoms of dementia be refused, this guideline is not uniformly followed. In the summer of 1995, the FDA issued interim recommendations regarding plasma-based products derived from donors diagnosed with, or at known high risk for, CJD. This was done at the insistence of members of the hemophilia community, who had watched in horror when a clotting-factor lot was withdrawn from the market because a donor had died of CJD.

The prion that is suspected of causing CJD is extremely small (less than one hundred nanometers). It cannot be inactivated by heat, gamma radiation, ultraviolet light, or formaldehyde, but it is susceptible to autoclaving (heating in a pressure-cooker-type sterilizer) at 132 degrees Celsius and 15 pounds of pressure per square inch for one hour or by immersion for one hour in household bleach. Unfortunately, these processes destroy blood components, so they cannot be used to protect blood products from CJD.

CJD is extremely rare, and the blood-banking industry cannot pressure-cook blood or soak it in chlorine bleach to eliminate the risk of passing on something so exotic. But it can and should do more to prevent the transmission of the most common blood-borne viral illnesses. Dr. Roger Dodd of the American Red Cross claims that the "objective of a zero-risk blood supply is virtually unachievable." That may be true. But we should be able to do better than we are doing now, especially when the means exist to destroy the most common viruses–and many uncommon ones as well.

––––––––––

In fact, it should soon be possible to vastly improve blood safety. According to Dr. Bernard Horowitz, a research scientist at Melville Biologics, a subsidiary of the New York Blood Center, a plasma treated with a solvent detergent has been developed. Although it is derived from pooling the plasma of many donors, it is virally inactivated and is said to be not only just as effective as single-donor fresh-frozen plasma but also safer. Dr. Horowitz reports that it eliminates the risk of transmitting hepatitis B, hepatitis C, and HIV, and it decreases the incidence of posttransfusion fever. Clinical trials of this product in the United States have been extremely successful. The virally inactivated plasma is widely used in Europe. It accounts for 30 to 50 percent of the plasma used in France, and in Norway it is the only form of transfusion plasma used.

Melville Biologics is also involved in developing a program for virally inactivating the cellular parts of whole blood, which would reduce and possibly eliminate graft-versus-host reaction. This occurs when a healthy T-cell is transfused into a patient who is immunologically incompetent. The transfused, or "grafted," T-cell attacks the host and causes a reaction that results in severe illness and sometimes death. The patients who are most at risk for graft-versus-host reaction are the same patients who are usually most in need of a transfusion: cancer and leukemia patients receiving chemotherapy, lupus patients, transplant patients, aplastic anemia patients, AIDS patients. The virally inactivated cellular products can mean the difference between life and death for them.

Viruses are composed of nucleic acid, a capsid, or protein coat, and in some cases a fatty envelope. HIV and hepatitis B and C are "enveloped" viruses. A solvent detergent inactivates enveloped viruses by dissolving their fatty envelopes. Nonenveloped viruses, such as the B-19 parvovirus and hepatitis A virus, can be inactivated by UV-C, a type of ultraviolet ray that is absorbed by nucleic acid. Plasma treated with UV-C as well as with a solvent detergent could result in a virus-free blood product.

Dr. Horowitz believes that the New York Blood Center can virally inactivate enough plasma in the near future to meet the needs of the blood banks of small hospitals as well as the demands of the American Red Cross. But the question remains whether blood banks across the nation will rush to replace untreated blood products with new virally inactivated products.

The support of the blood banks is needed to encourage the industry to develop and implement procedures for virally inactivating plasma and other blood products. Ethics and concern for the well-being of the patient did not adequately motivate the manufacturers of clotting-factor concentrate to come up with a safer product, and it is unrealistic to expect corporate concern for the bottom line to change. The FDA's support is crucial here, too, but in the past the FDA's Blood Products Advisory Committee was top-heavy with industry representatives, and it is not surprising that its decisions have erred in favor of industry.

Cronyism between government agencies and industry was recognized as a danger by the Institute of Medicine, which in 1995 suggested that a blood-safety director at the level of a deputy assistant secretary or higher be named to the Department of Health and Human Services and that a blood-safety council be established. On October 12, 1995, just two months after the release of the Institute of Medicine report, Dr. Philip Lee was named Health and Human Services assistant secretary for health and head of the Blood Products Advisory Committee.

In response to the Institute of Medicine's recommendations, the FDA announced that BPAC would be restructured. The new BPAC consists primarily of voting members who are either specialists in hematology or representatives of government agencies and blood-product consumers. Skeptics fear that even a restructured BPAC will not destroy the "good old boy" network of the FDA and industry. The pharmaceutical and blood-banking industries eagerly recruit former FDA employees, and those presently within the FDA may not want to jeopardize plum positions that could be offered to them down the road. Nevertheless, it is hoped that the new BPAC will safeguard the future. But what of past wrongs? For decades, the manufacturers of clotting-factor concentrate earned huge profits at the expense of their customers' well-being. Should this injustice go unpunished? Should the companies be rewarded with still greater profits? Most states allow an injured party to file a lawsuit within two years of the date of injury or within two years of the date on which the injured party learned that damage occurred. The exceptions are cases of minors and cases of wrongful death. In the case of a minor, the statute of limitations takes effect when he or she reaches the age of majority or dies. In a case of wrongful death, the statute of limitations takes effect at the time of death, even if the deceased was not a minor when injured and the injury occurred years before. Few cases of hemophiliacs with HIV are within the statute of limitations.

In the summer of 1994, the Hemophilia Association of New Jersey began to seek sponsors of a Hemophilia Justice Act that would open a window in the statute of limitations for hemophiliacs who had become HIV-positive through the use of tainted blood products. Members of the association's ad hoc legislative committee contacted every state legislator, visited most of them, and repeatedly explained the urgent need for the bill. They had strong and wily opponents. The bill was opposed by Richard Weinroth, a lobbyist representing the American Blood Resources Association, and John Sheridan, a lobbyist representing Bayer. Sheridan had led Governor Christine Todd Whitman's transition team, and he wielded considerable political influence.

After a year of hard work, the bill reached the state senate and assembly floors. In the summer of 1995, the senate voted 38–0 in favor of the bill. The assembly voted 73–1 in favor. In the battle of wills with Governor Whitman that ensued, the attorney general's office suggested that the bill might be unconstitutional. Precedence in both the New Jersey Supreme Court and the U.S. Supreme Court suggested otherwise. Legal scholars believed the bill to be constitutional, and the New Jersey Bipartisan Office of Legislative Services agreed.

In a television interview, Governor Whitman said that she "really can't be signing unconstitutional bills," although she had strongly endorsed and signed other bills of questionable constitutionality. One such bill became Megan's Law, which was almost instantly introduced in the legislatures of other states. Though commendable in its effort to protect young children from convicted sex offenders, Megan's Law has traveled a rocky road in the courts. It has been repeatedly challenged as violating the First Amendment right to privacy. Megan's Law has been opposed principally by convicted sex offenders and their supporters, however, none of whom have much to offer in terms of political clout and campaign contributions. The Hemophilia Justice Act, on the other hand, was opposed by giant corporations, trade organizations, and powerful lobbyists.

The New Jersey Hemophilia Justice Act was of particular significance because if passed, it would establish a legal precedent for the introduction of a similar bill on the federal level; thus while they waited for the anticipated gubernatorial veto, New Jersey hemophiliacs were visibly frustrated. They began to get a lot of local press coverage, and in July 1995 held a rally in front of the statehouse in an attempt to gain public support.

A few days before the rally, Teddy and I sit in my office at home.

"I have to what?" he says.

"You don't have to do anything. You are being asked to write and present the prayer for the governor," I explain.

"But why me?"

"Because you are a hemophiliac with AIDS, because you lost two hemophilic brothers to AIDS, because you're the most handsome member of the association."

Teddy grins. "OK, I'll do it, but you have to help."

*We work out the wording of his prayer. It takes hours, but we fi-
nally produce something we think will be effective. At times, Teddy's
recommendations are highly irreverent: "Let us pray that Governor
Whitman isn't in the back pocket of the manufacturers," and so forth.*

"Let's be nice," I advise. "Let's give her the benefit of the doubt."

*Teddy raises his eyebrows. He is already politically jaded. "Yeah,
right," he says.*

*We try for a gentler prayer. I help Teddy couch his concerns more
delicately.*

*The day of the rally is beastly hot, yet hundreds of people gather. A
children's gospel choir sings. We stand holding posters and photos of
our lost loved ones. At the podium, the prayers begin.*

*First we read our eulogies. Erik speaks about Cubby. His voice
breaks. He cries.*

Teddy steps to the podium.

> *In our family there were five sons—two big kids and three little kids.
> I was one of the three little kids. Sometimes my mom used to call us
> the Three Musketeers. At other times, she would call us the three lit-
> tle pigs or the three bears, depending on how politely we acted, how
> dirty we were, or how boisterous our behavior was.*
>
> *I am the only surviving member of the three little kids. My
> brother Cubby, one year younger than me, died two years ago. My
> brother Mike, one year older than me, died one year ago.*
>
> *Now I am one of the big kids. The three little kids are no more. I
> could accept it if we all grew up and stopped being little kids—but
> the deaths—that I can't accept.*

*Erik and Teddy are followed by the parents and spouses of other he-
mophiliacs, who speak of their lost loved ones. Prayers are said, and
finally Teddy begins his prayer for the governor. I wonder at his
solemnity and dignity. Is this the same teenager who was giving me
such a hard time?*

> *Whether we be Christian, Muslim, Buddhist, Jew, Hindu, or any
> other religion in this country, let us take a few moments to bow our
> heads in prayer to whatever divine spirit guides us.*

Let us pray for Governor Whitman, ... that her character may be granted the strength to resist temptation–a temptation that must frequently come to an elected official–the temptation to make a decision based on the benefits it can offer a political career rather than the benefits it can bring to the people; ... that her heart be softened to feel the pain and sadness of the victims of this medically induced disaster and to feel the sorrow and grief of the loved ones left behind; ... that her mind be made flexible and capable of understanding that no human-made law is eternal, just as humans do not survive on this earth for all eternity; ... that her memory be jogged to recall that our founding fathers established three branches of our government–legislative, executive, and judicial–in order to establish a system of checks and balances; ... that her hands be guided to pick up her pen and sign our bill, a bill that will allow us to seek justice.

Let us observe a moment of silence and send our prayer on the wings of angels.

During that hot summer of 1995, Governor Whitman's heart was not softened. Her mind was not made flexible. Her memory was not jogged. Her hands were not guided. Her character–what can one say about character when the conditional veto of the Hemophilia Justice Act was written in collusion with the lobbyists representing the bill's opponents. This collusion was brought to the attention of the press by State Senator John Lynch, who on August 23, 1995, wrote an open letter to the press:

> Particularly galling is the issue of process. Over the summer and prior to meeting with representatives of the victims, the Governor's Chief Counsel met with representatives of the Offices of John Sheridan and Richard Weinroth, who represent different segments of the blood manufacturers industry. At that meeting, they discussed various ways to phrase the language of the veto. It was not until the day before the veto was announced, however, before that same office met with the victims. This meeting, if one could call it that, was nothing more than presenting the victims with a fait accompli, showing them the proposed language and

asking them if it was acceptable. Any concerns that the victims expressed at the meeting were not addressed in the final version of the veto.

Without a Hemophilia Justice Act, each HIV-positive victim would be forced to prove to a judge that his case was worthy of exemption from the statute of limitations or that he had become aware of his illness less than two years before filing his lawsuit.

Some cases would be treated justly, fairly, and compassionately. Others would not.

December 1995. Elena Bostick is on the phone, organizing a group of hemophiliacs to sing Christmas carols in front of the governor's mansion while a Christmas party for the legislators takes place.

"Oh, Elena. We're not expected to sing real Christmas carols, are we? We don't want Governor Whitman to think that we're entertaining her. Let me make up some carols."

Elena agrees to let me organize the singing, and she manages to persuade about thirty angry members of the Hemophilia Association of New Jersey to brave the elements.

At the governor's mansion, Drumthwacket, we gather in a shivering cluster. Though the night is bitterly cold, our fury keeps us warm, and we belt out our carols.

> *Away in a mansion the governor sleeps.*
> *No deathbed vigil of sons does she keep.*
> *Her loved ones aren't wasting a bit every day,*
> *While lobbyists earn their blood-tainted pay.*
> *Away in a mansion the governor wakes,*
> *Facing each morning without the heartaches*
> *Of knowing an industry just didn't care*
> *Enough for the safety of loved ones most dear.*

Christmas and New Year's Day came and went. The New Jersey hemophilia community plotted and planned, showing up at the statehouse in fine weather and foul.

At five-thirty one morning, I was bundling comforters around Teddy as he curled up in the backseat of the car to sleep away the trip to Trenton. Erik cleared a foot of snow off the windshield of my car as I loaded up the hot beverages and snacks. What was being called the blizzard of the century howled around us. It was the last day of the 205th legislative session, and if the governor's veto of our bill wasn't overridden today, the bill would die.

Teddy, Erik, and I were the vanguard of the New Jersey hemophilia community, because we were the only ones whose street had been plowed. State legislators were being transported to Trenton by state troopers in four-wheel-drive vehicles.

The three of us arrived at the statehouse even before the security guards, who exchanged greetings with us as they staggered in. We had become familiar figures. Teddy and Erik set up their chess pieces, and I kept watch for early arrivals. Many of the legislators smiled as they saw the boys intent on their chess game. They'd seen them play chess hundreds of times at the statehouse while waiting for hearings on our bill to commence.

I pounced on the legislators as they came through the door. The assemblywomen headed off to the ladies' room, and I followed them in and reminded them to support the bill. I was at a disadvantage with the male legislators, and I tried to persuade Erik or Teddy to follow them into the men's room, but they drew the line. "Look, Mom," Erik said. "We've sung Christmas carols and froze half to death. We've driven through a blizzard. We've sweltered at middle-of-the-summer rallies. We've sat for hours, sometimes bored to death, in voting chambers and committee rooms. We've written letters, made telephone calls, made speeches, and even allowed television cameras in our bedrooms, but we are not going to follow these guys into the men's room."

———————

The governor's veto was not overridden. Time ran out before our bill could be posted for a vote. But a slightly modified version of the original bill was introduced within days of the next session. The new bill stipulated that a two-year statute of limitations begin on July 13, 1995, the day the Institute of Medicine had released its report stating that clotting-factor concentrate could have been virally inactivated as early as 1980. Although a majority in the state senate and the state assembly signed on as sponsors, the bill's passage was not assured. There were many new faces in both houses, and some old friends of the Hemophilia Association of New Jersey had not been reelected. The hemophilia community needed to sell the worthiness of its bill to the new legislators while the blood-industry lobbyists were trying to turn them against the bill.

In the course of lobbying, John Sheridan portrayed his client, Bayer, as the victim of hemophiliacs who had played on sympathy to "trample the rights of others." Sheridan attempted to solicit the support of the New Jersey State Senate Judiciary Committee by asking its members to "apply the concept of this bill to your own lives. What if you, or the other people in this room, were to wake up and find that you were being sued today for an accident that took place in 1983?" Sheridan neglected of course to explain that the issue at hand did not involve an accident. It was the tragic consequence of policies established to enhance financial profit.

Sheridan described as "disingenuous" the hemophiliacs' fear of being discriminated against for their HIV-positive status even though Cutter, which is owned by Bayer and represented by Sheridan, had persuaded the National Hemophilia Foundation in 1985 to oppose a class-action suit against the companies that sold HIV-infected products. The justification was that such a suit would encourage "irrational discrimination." Effectively intimidated by the NHF's stance, the majority of patients allowed the statute of limitations to expire. In light of this, Sheridan's 1995 testimony before the New Jersey State Senate Judiciary Committee on behalf of Bayer was itself outrageously disingenuous.

The Hemophilia Justice Act was passed in the New Jersey State Senate on March 21, 1996, with a vote of 38–0. It was passed in the New Jersey State Assembly on May 6, 1996, with only one abstention and one dissenting vote. Governor Whitman signed the bill two days later, leaving many members of the community perplexed about the motive behind her veto earlier. The Hemophilia Justice Act allegedly had not been favored by the Republican National Committee, and by signing the bill Whitman risked paying a high political price. Perhaps Teddy's prayer was answered. Perhaps the governor was granted the strength to resist the temptation of potential campaign donations and the ire of her supporters.

————

Winning one battle does not guarantee the outcome of the war. Hemophiliacs face a fierce struggle in the forty-seven states with statutory blood-shield laws. Statutes of limitations should be scrutinized in every state, and not just with regard to the hemophilia-HIV issue. Most such statutes are a century old. They were passed when scientists had no concept of viruses, let alone viruses with incubation periods of seven to ten years or more.

Blood-shield laws should be amended or abolished. In Minnesota, when an attempt was made to emulate the success of the Hemophilia Association of New Jersey, clotting-factor manufacturers hired thirty lobbyists to defeat the proposed legislation. Protecting nonprofit blood banks that rely on volunteer donors is understandable, but protecting a multibillion-dollar for-profit industry from strict product liability is absurd. In 1985, an amendment to California's blood-shield law was proposed whereby manufactured blood components, including clotting factor, would be reclassified as salable products, not services. But California's blood-shield law remains unchanged. The plasma-fractionating industry is still exempt from strict product liability. There is no excuse for this, since all manufactured intravenous and injectible products derived from plasma components could be virally inactivated.

If the hemophilia community does not succeed in affecting legislative changes nationwide and if blood-shield statutes are permitted to stand, then the nation's blood supply might never be safe. The political machine is too strongly linked to corporate dollars for a small group of hemophilia survivors to accomplish everything that needs to be done, but if more people understand that what is at stake affects them and their children, too, then perhaps the horror that has been visited on hemophiliacs will not continue or be repeated in some other permutation.

People should familiarize themselves with the legislative process and know whom their legislators really represent. The Election Law Enforcement Commission will, for a small fee, tell you who has donated what to a candidate's campaign. If a legislator is accepting large campaign contributions from "the enemy," a citizen needs to know this.

The press and television wield the greatest power in a battle for legislation. Public opinion counts for a lot. The battle for New Jersey's Hemophilia Justice Act was fought in newspapers throughout the state. Every opportunity the community found for media attention, it took. The satiric Christmas carols, sung on that bitter December night, ended up appearing in David Preston's *Philadelphia Inquirer* column–two days in a row. New Jersey hemophiliacs were so vociferous that their efforts were even reported in the respected British medical journal *The Lancet.*

Changing laws and the way lawmakers think takes a lot of time and a lot of hard work. One can let the other guy worry about the blood-shield laws and the safety of the nation's blood supply, but it may not be the other guy or the other guy's child who's going to need the transfusion.

CHAPTER 12

In the Darkness of Grief

I WANTED TO DIE AFTER THE DEATHS OF MY SONS. KNOWING THAT MY family needed me wasn't enough to get me out of bed in the morning. But I had promised Cubby that I would continue his fundraising and public-education efforts, and that as well as my own need to have the deaths of my boys count for something led me in directions I would never have thought myself capable of going.

I developed a terrible rage because I knew my children need not have died. They shouldn't even have been exposed to hepatitis, let alone AIDS. Once I felt this rage, I realized that living with anger is less painful than living with grief. Anger energized me whereas grief drained me. I began to write this book, and at the same time I threw my heart and soul into the Hemophilia Association of New Jersey's legislative efforts to gain a waiver in the statute of limitations for lawsuits brought by hemophiliacs with HIV.

On a late-summer night in 1995, I picked up Cubby's handwritten memoirs. I had been putting off this moment, but I had promised Cubby that I would not let him be forgotten. I opened his loose-leaf binder and faced a sea of gaily colored pages full of joy and promise. I took the first page of single-spaced, college-ruled paper and propped it by my keyboard. Squinting, I tried to decipher Cubby's tiny, curly cursive. Then I began to type. It took me two weeks to transcribe the handwritten memoirs onto the hard drive of my computer. During those two weeks, I felt as if Cubby were sitting close by me. I laughed and cried buckets, but I felt an incredible sense of closeness to my son.

I have many wonderful memories of my boys but also many painful and angry memories. Sometimes the painful memories haunt me and keep me awake until all hours of the night. Cubby was a sweet, compassionate, funny, and charismatic child. He was very popular in school, and because of the wonderful education that the school nurse provided to everyone, no one there feared his AIDS. The situation was different in our neighborhood, however.

While my family was suffering from the pain of watching the children weaken and die, some of our neighbors cruelly harassed the boys. Many fine people in our neighborhood were fond of the children and supported Cubby's charitable activities, but a few caused us much sadness. Our pet rabbits were poisoned. Someone took an ax to the rabbit hutch. Someone poisoned our three-month-old puppy while he was romping in our fenced-in yard. Our cars were damaged at night. One year every letter mailed to us from the high school was stolen, torn open, and then returned to us. Luckily for us, each stolen letter announced an award or special recognition for Adam or Erik.

Teddy and Cubby were excluded from neighborhood play. Some children called them names. I remember when a neighbor's little boy would endlessly beg Cubby to cross the street and play with him. Every time Cubby did so, the child's father would shout, "Go away, get out of here." Crestfallen, Cubby would return home. I especially recall one particular afternoon when Cubby explained to his little friend that he couldn't play with him. "Your father chases me home as soon as I get there," he said, exasperated. "Go ask him why he chases me home." The boy ran into his house, but soon returned to the curb and said forlornly, "My daddy said you can't play with me because he hates your guts." What an ugly message for a father to give his young son. I remember when a neighbor installed a basketball hoop by the curb. Teddy, who had already lost Mike and Cubby by then, would look longingly at the children as they played basketball. By this time, he was too intimidated to ask to play, but one afternoon he brought his basketball outside and began to shoot baskets. The father who had installed the basketball hoop chased him away. Everybody else was allowed to play there, but not Teddy.

I remember bringing Cubby to the county courthouse shortly before he died. I wouldn't leave him home because he was afraid he would die without me beside him. I couldn't stay home with him because we were being sued by a neighbor for using a ventilation fan that was required by our township's building code and was well within the required noise-ordinance limits. Eventually the judge recognized that there was a problem that went beyond the fan. In his decision, he stated that the case "clearly bespoke of bigotry . . . unrebutted in its ugly form." Though we won the case, it cost us thirty thousand dollars to defend ourselves.

After Cubby's and Mike's deaths, my friend Julie told me about her experience in the neighborhood. Her family had moved there during the summer of 1989. Her shy little boy, Scott, was instantly drawn to Cubby. They became best of friends that summer, but Julie was warned by some of the neighborhood parents not to let her children play with any of my sons. "They have hemophilia, so they must have AIDS," was the reasoning. "The little one is always sick. We've told our children, 'When Teddy and Cubby come to play, you are to come into the house.' "

The love and devotion so many people demonstrated toward my children is something I think about often. Unfortunately, the mean-spiritedness and discrimination is also something I think about often.

Charles, my husband, has suffered in a unique way. His suffering comes not only from the loss of his sons but also from the loss of his identity. I believe this came about as an indirect result of AIDS in our lives.

For more than twenty years, Charles worked for the same company. It often changed owners, but Charles had a fine reputation and was appreciated by one parent company after another. Then, in 1994, Charles and I filed three lawsuits against the manufacturers of clotting-factor concentrate, and from 1994 to 1996, I opposed lobbyists for these manufacturers in my efforts in behalf of New Jersey's Hemophilia Justice Act. The most powerful lobbyist opposing this legislation represented the Bayer Corporation, one of the largest customers serviced by the business group for which Charles worked as a director of operations. I suspected that at some point Charles's career might suffer from our lawsuit, my political activities, or this book. He was certain it wouldn't. Unfortunately, I seem to have been proved right.

On January 24, 1996, Elena Bostick, the executive director of the Hemophilia Association of New Jersey, gave a deposition to the attorneys representing the clotting-factor manufacturers, and she identified me as the provider of many of the documents she had used in her testimony before the committees of the New Jersey State Senate and State Assembly. When the attorneys for the plasma fractionators commented on the number of documents I possessed, Elena misinterpreted their remark as a question and told them that I had used these documents in the writing of a book.

Charles's job had not previously been threatened, but all that changed immediately after Elena's deposition. Representatives from his company began to make frequent visits to his plant, following workers and photographing them at their jobs. Charles had no idea what had suddenly precipitated such blatantly hostile surveillance.

On February 15, 1996, I testified before the New Jersey State Senate Judiciary Committee, and on February 22, I testified before the State Assembly Judiciary Committee regarding the role of the plasma-fractionating industry in the transmission of HIV to New Jersey's hemophiliacs. Four days later Charles's direct supervisor at his company's divisional level discussed with him the "unacceptable performance" of his plant.

On February 20, I was quoted by *The Star-Ledger*, a northern New Jersey newspaper, as saying, "It is unfair to expect the government and taxpayers to pay for this disaster when the manufacturers are at fault." I said that "lawsuits are the best way to hold the manufacturers accountable." On February 29, Charles was placed on thirty-days probation by his company.

Charles was stunned by the content and tone of the February 29 memo. During the previous three years, he had been involved in locating and negotiating for a new manufacturing site. He had arranged for the contracting and building of a new manufacturing facility. According to one company executive, this facility was exceptionally well organized despite the fact that just months before Charles had moved eight different manufacturing processes from several different plants into the new megafacility. It became apparent to Charles that his company was making an effort to establish "cause" in order to fire him. In addition, it was requiring that he conform to standards of performance different from those of operations managers at other facilities.

On March 4, the attorney for Miles (Bayer) demanded that I produce my manuscript "for inspection and copying." On March 5, the *Trenton County Times*, a central New Jersey daily newspaper, published an op-ed piece that I had written. The piece was critical of the plasma-fractionating industry. On March 18, my attorney informed the representatives of the clotting-factor manufacturers that I refused to present my manuscript for inspection and copying. On March 25, Charles received another memo that artlessly and feebly attempted to build a case for termination of employment on the basis of cause. In it, he was informed that he was still on probation. On March 29, the *Asbury Park Press* published an op-ed piece I had written that highlighted the role of the clotting manufacturers in the hemophilia-HIV tragedy.

In early April, a university press offered me a contract for *Cry Bloody Murder*. On the same day, Random House made its bid for the book. On the very next business day, Charles was fired and given a four-week special assignment in lieu of notice. During the month of Charles's "special assignment," I opposed an offer made by the manufacturers to HIV-infected hemophiliacs, because I believed that a settlement of $100,000 per HIV-infected individual was inadequate. Teddy and I voiced our objections during an interview on a nationally broadcast cable news program. Following the television appearance, representatives from Charles's company's divisional headquarters and its corporate headquarters contacted people at his facility, requesting copies of the newspapers in which I was featured for my "charitable activities."

Charles was always the good team player and an excellent manager. On the morning of Cubby's death, he had driven to his divisional headquarters in North Jersey in an effort to prevent the relocation of his facility to a site eight hundred miles away. He was concerned with the well-being of his employees, most of them unskilled and financially unable to relocate. Charles convinced himself that when he came home that evening, Cubby would be sitting up watching television. Instead, I had to telephone his office to inform him of his son's death. Shortly before he died, Cubby had asked, "Where's Daddy?" I had to explain that Daddy was trying to save his employees' jobs. Cubby's final message to his father was "Tell Daddy that I understand. I wouldn't want those people to be out of work. Then they couldn't buy food for their children."

Cubby had understood, but to this day his father does not understand. He has never forgiven himself for not being there when Cubby died. Charles's guilt for not being there for Cubby worsened when after more than twenty years of excellent performance reviews and exceptional service, he lost his job. He was fired without severance pay. Reports of poor performance were fabricated but disproved by company executives who contacted him after his termination. Charles said to me, "I'm in my fifties. I worked hard for them for more than twenty years. Why did they just take me out and shoot me like an old horse?"

Erik graduated from high school two weeks after Cubby's death. He won every art prize awarded by his school. He spent the summer illustrating one of Cubby's books. Though he had been accepted by the School of Visual Arts in Manhattan, he deferred admission because of Mike's worsening condition. When Mike died just nine months after Cubby, Erik found it even more difficult to leave home. He said, "Not so long ago there were five loud, active boys in this house. I can't go away and leave Teddy alone." Erik saw Teddy through some pretty tough times. Now, with Teddy's health stable, Erik will major in cartooning at the School of Visual Arts.

At a rally held in memory of New Jersey hemophiliacs who had died of AIDS, Erik spoke of Cubby:

> My little brother Cubby and I loved cartooning. He used to say to me, "If there was some miracle drug to cure AIDS and I grew up, you and I could go into business together. You could do the drawing and inking, and I would be your colorist. We'd make a great team. Our business cards would say DEPRINCE BROTHERS—CARTOONING AND GRAPHIC ARTS.
>
> My brother died of AIDS two years ago, when he was eleven years old. We will never go into business together. Now I must do the cartooning all by myself—the drawing, the inking, and the coloring. This is my career, and there is never a moment when I am working that I don't miss Cubby.

Cubby had said to me before he died, "Mom, when I die, Adam is going to want to skip his GREs. Please make him go." As Cubby predicted, Adam woke up on the morning of his Graduate Record Examination, two days after Cubby died, sobbing and refusing to take the exam. I begged him to go and told him what Cubby had said. Adam took the tests and scored 790 in analysis and 750 in math, out of a possible score of 800. He was accepted directly by New Jersey Institute of Technology's PhD Program in Computer Science.

For a very long time after the deaths of Cubby and Mike, Adam found it painful to come home. He told me that he always expected Cubby to be waiting for him at the door, eager to run down the driveway and jump into his arms. He expected to spend time with Mike at his computer, teaching him to program. As long as he was away from home, Adam could pretend that his brothers were still alive. Returning home was a harsh reminder of the reality he didn't want to face.

Adam was afraid that if he came home, someone would die. He had come home for summer break in 1993, and Cubby died shortly afterward. He returned home for the winter break a few days before Christmas of 1993, and Cubby's beloved dog, Stripe, died. Then he returned home three months later, for spring break of 1994, and Mike died.

It was only after Adam became engaged to be married that he was able, with the help of his fiancée, to cope with the loss of his brothers. By the time he was married, in August of 1996, he was able to allow himself to feel close to Teddy. Now he and his wife, Melissa, visit frequently. Adam no longer fears bringing death home with him, but he is still often unable to talk about Mike and Cubby.

Teddy has worked hard to stay well. It hasn't been easy for him. The medications he has taken over the last few years have taken their toll. One drug made him anorectic. Another caused unrelenting abdominal pain, diarrhea, and nausea. One drug caused such a severe lassitude that he appeared to have developed AIDS dementia. He was unable to concentrate. He got lost. He forgot which season of the year it was. Teddy once admitted to me that it was easier to accept a detention for skipping a class than admit to the teacher that he had no idea where he was.

Life has improved a great deal for Teddy. He takes a new combination of drugs. His memory has returned. He is doing well in school again, and he's active in extracurricular activities. Ted is far shier than Cubby ever was. He lacks his younger brother's natural ease with people and gift of gab. He is a more private person than Cubby. Yet he feels a sense of responsibility to carry on Cubby's work. Teddy willingly allows himself to be interviewed by television reporters and the press. He may hate every second of the interview, but he smiles anyway.

Teddy speaks to other young people about AIDS. Sometimes he will tell them about his own experiences. Sometimes he tells them about Mike's death. Often he reads from something Cubby wrote shortly before he died.

64 Reasons Why
You Do Not Want
to Get AIDS
by
Charles John "Cubby" DePrince, Jr.

1. You have to take so many pills that your stomach feels filled up with pills and you don't feel like eating your dinner.
2. The pills make you feel tired.
3. The pills give you a headache.
4. Some of the pills make you feel like you have to throw up, so you carry a vomit bucket all around with you.
5. You get oral thrush in your mouth and down your throat and the pain is so bad that every time you swallow it feels like you swallowed a rusty Brillo.
6. Oral thrush makes your tongue look gross.
7. Your taste buds don't work right, so your food tastes weird.
8. You get shingles. They are blisters that go around your body in a circle. They make your back hurt so much that you have to be hunched over, and when you get covered with a sheet, it feels like somebody is stabbing you.
9. You get pneumonia lots of times and you can't breathe.
10. You get scared because you can't breathe and you feel like you are suffocating.
11. You get lots of high fevers.
12. You get chills.
13. Your eyes get infected and swollen shut and yucky white stuff oozes out and then your eyes get glued shut.
14. You get ugly rashes on your arms.
15. The rashes itch like crazy.
16. You get an ugly fungus under your fingernails.
17. The fungus itches and hurts because it pushes on your nails, so you bite your nails to make them feel better.
18. Your hair falls out.
19. Your medicines make your teeth turn black.
20. You get gingivitis and your teeth get loose.
21. You don't grow.
22. You get diarrhea most of the time.

23. Your brain shrinks and you sometimes forget what you are talking about, and suddenly you forget how to write cursive.

24. Sometimes people get paralyzed, like my brother Mike.

25. When you get paralyzed, your face is stuck one way and you can't make a good smile.

26. When you get paralyzed, you choke on your food.

27. You lose your balance.

28. Your bone marrow stops working and you have to get Neupogen injections every other day.

29. You get the injections in your stomach on some days.

30. The Neupogen injections give you bad pains in your bones.

31. The pains in your bones make you feel like an old person.

32. You get infections in your bloodstream and have to get IV antibiotics every day.

33. You have to get heparin locks put in your veins so that you can get the IV antibiotics.

34. Some of the IV antibiotics burn your veins and you get really bad pain in your arms and they swell up.

35. Some of the IV antibiotics give you bad rashes all over your body and when you go outside, all of the fruit flies follow you around so you can't even enjoy a picnic.

36. You get herpes infection in your bloodstream and it makes sores in your mouth and throat and esophagus and the pain is horrible.

37. You have to gargle with some stuff that numbs your herpes sores and it also numbs your throat, so your saliva goes down the wrong tube and you choke.

38. You get a bird infection called MAI.

39. MAI infects all the organs in your body and you have pain every day in lots of places.

40. MAI makes your intestines swell shut so you can't eat. Then you have to get a broviac, which is a tube that goes in your chest and into your heart.

41. MAI infects your heart muscle. The heart muscle gets stiff and you feel very tired and breathless.

42. You get heart failure and your face and stomach swell up.

43. You get tumors in your liver.

44. You can't have surgery or chemotherapy for the tumors because you are already too sick with AIDS and the chemotherapy will make your immune system weaker.

45. You can't get radiation on your tumors because radiation makes your immune system weaker.

46. Your liver gets so big that you look like you swallowed a watermelon.

47. If your liver gets too big, you can't lie down to sleep at night or your heart and lungs get crushed.

48. If your liver gets too big, you can't sit up during the day or your heart and lungs get pushed up too far.

49. If your liver gets too big, then you have to sit half lying down and half sitting up. Then it's hard to paint your model airplanes because the paint drips on your stomach.

50. When your heart is failing and your liver is gigantic, it is hard to breathe because your lungs are filled with liquid and they are getting crushed all at the same time, so you feel like a hippopotamus is sitting on you.

51. You have to go to the hospital outpatient department and get packed red blood cells because you are too anemic and your heart beats about two hundred times a minute.

52. With a watermelon belly, skinny arms and legs, black teeth, and hair that's falling out, and being pushed around in a special reclining wheelchair, people stare at you in the mall, so you have to stick your tongue out at them when your parents aren't looking.

53. You miss your old bed that your dad made for you when you were little, because now you have to sleep in a hospital bed so that you can sit partway up to breathe.

54. You feel embarrassed when you wet your bed, even though your mom says it's OK, not to worry because she feels like putting some cheerful, clean sheets on the bed anyway, and you know that's not true because a mother would be crazy to want to change sheets in the middle of the night.

55. You have to make a will and decide who to leave all of your treasures to, especially your favorite teddy bear that your mom and dad bought you when you were four years old.

56. You worry about whether your dog will be OK when you die.

57. You think about what it would be like to grow up, but you know you won't.

58. You worry that when you die and go to heaven, you will miss your mom and dad and brothers. You worry even more that they will miss you and be sad.

59. You wonder if anybody will be named Charles John De-Prince III and if he will be called Cubby. You hope so.

60. You wonder if it is painful to die.

61. You make your mom promise to give you enough morphine when you are dying so that you don't feel any pain.

62. You do a lot of important things because you have to squeeze them into a short time like ten or eleven years instead of eighty-seven.

63. You try to be extra good and cheerful because if you are extra good and cheerful when you go to heaven, you'll get to be a guardian angel. Being a guardian angel is a better job than just being a spirit.

64. You wonder if people will still remember you after you are dead.

SOURCE NOTES

CHAPTER 1: *Love of Blood*

The primary source of medical information in this and other chapters is the second edition of *Clinical Hematology and Fundamentals of Hemostasis,* edited by Denise M. Harmening (Philadelphia: F. A. Davis, 1992). The National Hemophilia Foundation has for many years provided me with information on hemophilia and von Willebrand disease, and symposia sponsored by the Hemophilia Association of New Jersey have added to my knowledge. The description of what it is like to live with a coagulopathy is based on my own experiences raising my sons and the experiences of my friends and acquaintances in the hemophilia community.

Other published sources of information for this chapter include:

Armour Pharmaceutical Company. *Understanding Hemophilia: A Young Person's Guide.* Armour Pharmaceutical Company, 1991.

Eckert, Enid. *Your Child and Hemophilia.* New York: National Hemophilia Foundation, 1983.

Kee, K. L., ed. *Professional Guide to Diseases.* Springhouse, Pa.: Crossroad Publishing, 1991.

LaFon, Jill. *Exploring von Willebrand Disease.* New York: National Hemophilia Foundation, 1995.

Massie, Robert K. *Nicholas and Alexandra.* New York: Atheneum, 1972.

Montgomery, Robert, et al. *Understanding von Willebrand Disease.* New York: National Hemophilia Foundation, 1991.

Roher, Susan. "The Other Bleeding Disorder." *Hemalog* 5 (1994): 12.

Rosver, F. "Hemophilia in the Talmud and Rabbinic Writings." *Annals of Internal Medicine* 70 (1968): 833.

CHAPTER 3: *Treatment*

Conversations with hematologists and other physicians regarding their experiences with early and current hemophilia treatment provide the backbone of this chapter. Of special interest are the difficulties experienced by hemophiliacs seeking emergency room treatment. Dr. Alice Cohen, professor of pediatrics and a pediatric hematologist at the Newark, New Jersey, Beth Israel Medical Center, gave me valuable insights into the lack of instruction in coagulopathy available to medical students and how this affects the ability of emergency room staff and general practitioners to recognize and treat coagulopathy disorders. I gained additional insight into this problem from health care professionals who served with me on a 1994 New Jersey Department of Health Ad Hoc Committee Regarding Emergency Room Services for Children/Adults with Hemophilia or Sickle Cell Disease.

The names used here to refer to the manufacturers of blood-clotting-factor concentrates—Alpha, Armour, Baxter, and Bayer—are the names as they appear in court documents for the 1993 federal class-action suit *Wadleigh et al. v. Rhône-Poulenc Rorer et al.* (MDL-986), filed in the United States District Court for the Northern District of Illinois, Eastern Division. The principal defendants are Alpha Therapeutic Corporation, Green Cross of America Corporation, and The Green Cross Corporation (referred to collectively as Alpha); Armour Pharmaceutical Company and Rhône-Poulenc

Rorer, Incorporated (referred to collectively as Armour); Baxter Healthcare Corporation and Baxter International, Incorporated (collectively, Baxter, which also refers to Travenol Laboratories, Incorporated, and Hyland Therapeutics, a division of Baxter Healthcare Corporation); and Bayer Corporation and Bayer Atkiengessellschaft (collectively, Bayer, which also refers to Cutter Laboratories, Incorporated; Cutter Laboratories, a division of Miles, Incorporated; Miles Laboratories, Incorporated; Miles, Incorporated; and Miles Incorporated).

Published sources of information for this chapter include:

Agle, David, et al. *Home Therapy for Hemophilia.* New York: National Hemophilia Foundation, 1977.

Biggs, Rosemary, et al. "Can Hemophilia Patients Be Adequately Maintained with Cryoprecipitates? Or Is It Desirable or Even Necessary to Manufacture and Administer Highly Concentrated AHF Products?" *Vox Sang* 22 (1972): 554–565.

Drees, Thomas C. *Blood Plasma: The Promise and the Politics.* Port Washington, N.Y.: Ashley Books, 1983.

Ingram, G.I.C. "The History of Haemophilia." *Journal of Clinical Pathology* 29 (1995): 469–478.

Kasper, Carolyn K., et al. "Recent Evolution of Clotting Factor Concentrates for Hemophilia A and B." *Journal of the American Blood Resources Association,* summer 1993: 44–56.

Starr, Douglas. "Again and Again in World War II: Blood Made the Difference." *Smithsonian,* March 1995: 125–138.

CHAPTER 4: *Trade-off*

There are many accounts of the problem of vaccine-borne hepatitis B during World War II, but I discovered the story in Peter Radetsky's *The Invisible Invaders: The Story of the Emerging Age of Viruses* (Boston: Little, Brown, 1991). At about the same time, the subject came up in a conversation I had with Dr. Oscar Ratnoff, a hematologist and researcher at the University Hospitals of Cleveland. Dr. Ratnoff's pre–World War II research focused on liver disease and led him to be wary of the problems associated with pooled plasma products. It was Dr. Ratnoff who introduced me to the dusty bottle of Cohn Fraction I on the shelf of his laboratory (see Chapter 9), and he told me about his futile efforts to steer consumers away from clotting-factor concentrate.

My understanding of the exigencies of clotting-factor manufacturing was elucidated by Dr. Edward Shanbrom, who was involved in the development of the first FDA-approved clotting-factor concentrate. Additional information came from Dr. Thomas Drees, former CEO of Alpha Therapeutics.

Corporate and personal communications and documents quoted or cited in this chapter were either used as evidence for the plaintiffs in hemophilia-HIV litigation, accessible as Freedom of Information Act documents, introduced as evidence in state legislative committees (especially in Arizona and California), or written to elected or appointed officials for public benefit and made available to the public by the writer.

Information regarding the World Health Organization's position on plasmapheresis was obtained from WHO documents, including press releases and agenda items generated by the Twenty-eighth World Health Assembly in May 1975.

In correspondence and various other documents, the late Dr. J. Garrott Allen of Stanford University made clear his position on using plasma collected from paid and prison donors. A source of information for this chapter was Dr. Allen's letter to Dr. Ian A. Mitchell, special assistant to the U.S. assistant secretary for Health and Scientific Affairs. Allen allowed this letter and others on the issue of paid donors to be used in hemophilia-HIV cases. Before his death, he testified as an expert witness in such cases. Dr. Allen's position is also documented in his June 18, 1972, "Written Testimony in Support of Amended (California) Assembly Bill–285." Risk rates of serum hepatitis from commercial and prison blood were documented by him in this testimony.

In her letter of April 30, 1974, to Charles C. Edwards, assistant secretary for Health, the late Dr. Judith Graham Pool of Stanford University recorded her opinion of the use of clotting-factor concentrate. This letter was written in response to the Federal Register Issue of March 8, 1974, regarding the proposed implementation plan for a new national blood policy and "the dangerous, wasteful and unethical purchase of plasma by pharmaceutical houses to provide Factor VIII concentrate."

Because doctors are required to report only AIDS and not its precursor, an HIV infection, there is no proof of the actual number of hemophiliacs who are HIV infected. For years, the hemophilia community has been estimating the number to be 10,000. The manufacturers of clotting factor estimated the number to range between 4,000 and 6,000. After receiving approximately 8,000 responses to a settlement offer, the manufacturers recognized that their original estimate was inaccurate. I have estimated the number of HIV-infected hemophiliacs in the United States to fall between 10,000 and 12,000. My estimate is based on statistics calculated jointly by the Centers for Disease Control and Prevention, the National Hemophilia Foundation, and the New Jersey State Department of Health. Though these statistics were calculated in 1992, they are still valid because U.S. hemophiliacs did not contract HIV after the mid-1980s. The estimate of 10,000 to 12,000 HIV-infected hemophiliacs is corroborated by applying to the overall U.S. hemophilia population an infection rate determined from a study published in 1994 by the *Journal of Acquired Immune Deficiency Syndromes.*

Most of the information on hepatitis in this and other chapters was obtained during the Liver Disease in Hemophilia Conference, March 3–5, 1995, in Atlanta, Georgia. It was sponsored by the National Hemophilia Foundation and the Centers for Disease Control.

Other sources of information for this chapter include:

Alter, Harvey. "Overview of the Natural History of Hepatitis C Virus Infection." Abstract presented at the Liver Disease in Hemophilia Conference.

Brightman, I. J., and R. F. Korns. "Homologous Serum Jaundice in Recipients of Pooled Plasma." *Journal of the American Medical Association* 127 (1945): 144.

Gellis, Sydney S., et al. "Chemical, Clinical, and Immunological Studies on the Products of Human Plasma Fractionation. XXXVI: Inactivation of the Virus of Homologous Serum Hepatitis in Solution of Normal Human Serum Albumin by Means of Heat." *Journal of Clinical Investigation* 27 (1948): 239–244.

Kasper, Carolyn K., et al. "Recent Evolution of Clotting Factor Concentrates for Hemophilia A and B." *Journal of the American Blood Resources Association,* Summer 1993: 44–56.

Kroner, Barbara L., et al. "HIV-I Infection Incidence Among Persons with Hemophilia in the United States and Western Europe 1978–1990." *Journal of Acquired Immune Deficiency Syndromes* 7 (1994): 279–286.

Nelson, Kenrad E., et al. "Blood and Plasma Donations Among a Cohort of Intravenous Drug Users." *Journal of the American Medical Association* (1990): 2194–2197.

Operskalski, Eva. "Prevalence and Incidence of Hepatitis C Virus Infection and Interaction with Other Viruses Among Hemophiliacs in the Transfusion Safety Study Group Represented." Abstract presented at the Liver Disease in Hemophilia Conference.

Pierce, Glenn F., et al. "The Use of Purified Clotting Factor Concentrates in Hemophilia: Influence of Viral Safety, Cost, and Supply on Therapy." *Journal of the American Medical Association* 261 (1989): 3434–3438.

Rakela, Jorge. "Treatment of Hepatitis C Infection: The Role of Transplantation." Abstract presented at the Liver Disease in Hemophilia Conference.

Seef, Leonard. "Hemophilia and Chronic Hepatitis C." Abstract presented at the Liver Disease in Hemophilia Conference.

Severo, Richard. "Impoverished Haitians Sell Plasma for Use in the U.S." *New York Times,* January 28, 1972.

Shaw, Donna. "How Blood Was Smuggled from AIDS-Ravaged Africa." *Philadelphia Inquirer,* December 22, 1995.

Shulman, Stanford T., John P. Phair, and Herbert M. Sommers. *The Biologic and Clinical Basis of Infectious Diseases,* 4th ed. Philadelphia: W. B. Saunders, 1992.

Spurling, N., et al. "The Incidence, Incubation Period, and Symptomatology of Homologous Serum Jaundice." *British Medical Journal* 1 (1946): 409.

Troisi, Catherine, et al. "Hepatitis C Infection and Chronic Hepatitis in Hemophiliacs." Abstract presented at the Liver Disease in Hemophilia Conference.

CHAPTER 5: *Disaster*

The July 6, 1982, letter from Dr. Bruce Lee Evatt to Dr. Louis M. Aledort quoted in this chapter has circulated widely among hemophiliacs in the United States and abroad, principally through a collection of documents entitled "The Trail of AIDS." This collection was compiled and reproduced for distribution by the Committee of Ten Thousand (COTT). COTT was founded by a group of HIV-infected hemophiliacs and their families. Its members have worked toward achieving justice for the hemophilic victims of contaminated blood products and ensuring a safer national blood supply.

The generally accepted number of hemophiliacs (with hemophilia A and B) in the United States in 1982 ranged from 16,000 to 20,000. These figures were based on the number of hemophiliacs enrolled in the national system of hemophilia treatment centers, with allowance for the estimated number of hemophiliacs who were treated outside this system by private hematologists.

Many of the memos referred to in this chapter were compiled by COTT. These include "The List of Invitees to the July 27, 1982, Meeting of the Public Health Service Committee on Opportunistic Infections in Patients with Hemophilia"; the "Summary Report" of the July 27, 1982, Public Health Service meeting; excerpts from the transcript of the December 4, 1982, FDA Blood Products Advisory Committee meeting; the January 6, 1983, recommendation of the

American Association of Blood Banks; and Dr. Donald Francis's memo regarding the results of the 1982–83 T-cell surveillance study on hemophiliacs and his recommendations on the findings.

National Hemophilia Foundation memos, bulletins, and advisories are from my personal files dating back to 1982. They were sent to me during the last two decades by the Hemophilia Association of New Jersey, of which I have been a member since 1981. Information regarding the involvement of blood-products manufacturers in National Hemophilia Foundation communications was obtained from evidence introduced in *Gary W. Cross et al. v. Cutter Biological et al.*, No. 91-09617, Civil District Court for the Parish of Orleans, state of Louisiana.

AIDS statistics from the 1980s are taken from the Centers for Disease Control's *Morbidity and Mortality Weekly Report.* The rate of HIV transmission from hemophiliacs to their spouses was presented at New Directions, a symposium sponsored by the Hemophilia Association of New Jersey on February 27, 1988. My notes from that meeting indicate a 25 percent rate of infection among wives of HIV-infected hemophiliacs. Like all other HIV figures, the rate of transmission to spouses is not exact. There are societal pressures against disclosure, and only AIDS, not HIV infection, must be reported to state departments of health. Wives of hemophiliacs are denied treatment for HIV in many hemophilia centers, and the hemophilia community loses these women personally and statistically after their husbands die. My contacts and confidential interviews with wives of hemophiliacs lead me to believe that 25 percent is not an exaggerated rate, though rates as low as 10 percent have been suggested.

Other published sources of information for this chapter include:

Leveton, Lauren B., et al., eds. *HIV and the Blood Supply: An Analysis of Crisis Decisionmaking.* Washington, D.C.: National Academy Press, 1995.

Shaw, Donna. "Efforts to Make Blood Products Safer Tied to Competitive Pressures." *Philadelphia Inquirer,* July 18, 1995.

Shilts, Randy. *And the Band Played On.* New York: St. Martin's Press, 1987.

CHAPTER 7: *To the Utmost of Your Power*

Most of the material in this chapter is based on interviews, conversations, and correspondence with hematologists working in federally funded hemophilia treatment centers. A representative of Plasma Alliance and admissions staffs of several medical schools also provided information and opinions for this chapter.

Published sources of information include the following:

Alter, Miriam. "Sexual, Household, and Perinatal Transmission of Hepatitis B and Hepatitis C Virus Infections." Abstract presented at Liver Disease in Hemophilia Conference.

Gorman, Christine. "AIDS: The Exorcists." *Time,* special issue, fall 1996: 64–66.

Shaw, Donna. "How Blood Was Smuggled from AIDS-Ravaged Africa." *Philadelphia Inquirer,* December 22, 1995.

CHAPTER 8: *While Rome Burned*

The corporate memos, minutes of meetings, and related material, including consumer-targeted corporate-sponsored magazines and newsletters, that are quoted in this chapter were introduced as evidence for the plaintiffs in hemophilia-HIV cases, including the federal class-action suit *Wadleigh et al. v. Rhône-Poulenc Rorer et al.,* MDL-986, U.S. Court of Appeals for the Seventh Circuit, Chicago, and the previously cited *Gary W. Cross et al. v. Cutter Biological et al.*

The findings in the laboratory report by Dr. Alfred M. Prince regarding research for Revlon Health Care at the Laboratory of Virology, Lindsley F. Kimball Research Institute (referred to as the Prince Report) were published in *The Lancet* in 1986. The Prince Report and the contents of the laboratory reports prepared for Revlon Health Care by Dr. M. E. Hrinda at the Meloy Laboratories, Incorporated (referred to as the Meloy Report) were included in the minutes of Armour Pharmaceutical's Recombinant DNA Steering Committee meeting of October 15, 1985. The contents of the two reports and Armour's committee-meeting minutes were reported in *The Philadelphia Inquirer* in October 1995.

The 80 percent correlation between AIDS and hepatitis B core antibody positivity is documented in *John Doe v. Cutter Biological, Inc., et al.* and *John Smith v. Cutter Biological, Inc., et al.* (1992), WL-175798, U.S. Court of Appeals for the Ninth Circuit, Hawaii. The 80 percent rate has been the subject of much debate, with rates ranging from 40 percent, presented by the plasma-fractionating industry, to 90 percent, argued for by the CDC.

I listened to Douglas Fuson's statement regarding the blood-shield laws while in court. For this chapter, it was copied from the transcript of the Petition for a Writ of Mandamus in the U.S. Court of Appeals for the Seventh Circuit, No. 94-3912, in the Matter of *Rhône-Poulenc, Rorer, Inc., et al.*

Published sources of information for this chapter include:

Shaw, Donna. "Firms Kept Quiet About Risk of AIDS in Medicine." *Philadelphia Inquirer*, October 5, 1995.

——. "Was U.S. Medicine Dumped?" *Philadelphia Inquirer*, October 6, 1995.

——. "Firm Did Not Act on AIDS Virus Warning." *Philadelphia Inquirer*, October 23, 1995.

Shilts, Randy. *And the Band Played On.* New York: St. Martin's Press, 1987.

CHAPTER 9: *The Blood-Shield Laws*

Some of the information on blood products that was included in this chapter was provided by Dr. Edward Shanbrom, Dr. Oscar Ratnoff, and Dr. Bruce Evatt, chief of the CDC's Hematological Diseases Branch. Personal perspectives on hemophilia-HIV lawsuits and the blood-shield laws were offered during conversations and interviews with Lisa and the late Fred Smith of Illinois and Karen Cross, the mother of Brad Cross, a seventeen-year-old hemophiliac who died of AIDS (*Gary W. Cross et al. v. Cutter Biological et al.*). Professional perspectives on the blood-shield laws and/or blood-borne-disease litigation were provided by Thomas Mull of the law firm Mull and Mull; Nat Ozman of the law offices of Anesi, Ozman, and Rodin; and Sherman E. Fein of the law firm Fein, Schulman, Resnic, Pearson, and Emond.

In order to write this chapter, I studied the product-liability laws of all fifty states and the District of Columbia and significant cases, using annotated statutes of each state and court reports. The summary of the March 4, 1971, meeting of the New Hampshire House Judiciary Committee and the transcript of the state Senate Judiciary Committee's meeting of April 13, 1971, provided a representative sample of the typical legislative proceedings that contributed to the passage of blood-shield laws.

The letter to the lawyer representing Costa Rican HIV-infected hemophiliacs was written by Duncan Barr of the law firm O'Connor, Dillon, and Barr to Sherman Fein on November 18, 1985. The concern of the California deputy district attorney regarding the placement of blood-shield legislation is documented in a June 8, 1955, letter from Deputy Attorney General Dan Kaufmann to Governor Goodwin Knight.

Published sources of information for this chapter include:

Aledort, Louis. "Put Disease in Perspective Says NHF Official." *ECHO*, May 29, 1983.

Biggs, Rosemary, et al. "Can Hemophiliac Patients Be Adequately Maintained with Cryoprecipitates? Or Is It Desirable or Even Necessary to Manufacture and Administer Highly Concentrated AHF Products?" *Vox Sang* 22 (1972): 554–565.

Carlton, Sue. "Jury Finds for Hemophiliac AIDS Victim's Family." *St. Petersburg Times,* January 23, 1993.

Conway, Chris, and Josh Goldstein. "How Corporations Help Pay for Political Conventions." *Philadelphia Inquirer,* June 5, 1996.

Gomperts, E. D., et al. "Hepatocellular Enzyme Patterns and Hepatitis B Virus Exposure in Multitransfused Young and Very Young Hemophilia Patients." *American Journal of Hematology* 11 (1981): 55–59.

Greif, Robert C. "Hospital and Blood Bank Liability to Patients Who Contract AIDS Through Blood Transfusions." *San Diego Law Review* 23 (1986): 875–896.

Knoles, George H., and Rixford K. Snyder, eds. *Readings in Western Civilization.* Philadelphia: J. B. Lippincott, 1960.

Sanderson, Bill. "Blood Banks Group Must Pay Award in Transfusion Suit." *Bergen County Record,* June 6, 1995.

Starr, Douglas. "Again and Again in World War II: Blood Made the Difference." *Smithsonian,* March 1995: 125–138.

Westfall, Pamela T. "Hepatitis, AIDS, and the Blood Product Exemption from Strict Products Liability in California: A Reassessment." *Hastings Law Journal* 37 (1986): 1101–1132.

CHAPTER 10: *Loss and Compensation*

Morton C. Berkowitz of the Health Care Financing Administration, Beneficiary Services Branch, Division of Medicare, told me in 1989 that the Health Care Financing Administration considered hemophilia the most expensive of the catastrophic diseases. Optimal medical care for AIDS costs a fraction of comparable care for hemophilia, as I know from my own experience.

Conversations and interviews with hundreds of HIV-infected hemophiliacs and their families have shaped my views on the issue of compensation. Their feelings conform with my own family's experiences of loss and emotional frustration that stem from the manufacturers' failure to compensate victims and their families adequately and from the resulting lack of closure. My ongoing conversations with the Rilott family of Illinois have provided me with some of the most intimate and moving insights into the problem.

Information on compensation outside the United States was provided by the World Federation of Hemophilia Information Clearinghouse, the Canadian Hemophiliac Society, the Hemophilia Association of New Jersey, news broadcasts, and a *Philadelphia Inquirer* article about Japanese compensation of hemophiliacs with HIV. In the United States, legislative precedents for special benefits and financing based on health status or government or industry actions are available from the Congressional Research Service, in Washington, D.C.

Judge Richard A. Posner's statements and references to his role in the hemophilia-HIV class-action decertification are based on his March 16, 1995, decision in the the Seventh Circuit Court of Appeals, In the Matter of *Rhône-Poulenc, Rorer, Incorporated et al.:* Petition for a Writ of Mandamus.

Other published sources of information for this chapter include the following:

Shaw, Donna. "Maker of HIV-Tainted Drug to Pay Its Japanese Victims." *Philadelphia Inquirer,* February 27, 1996.

CHAPTER 11: *Risks and Regulation*

Product monographs on monoclonal and recombinant clotting-factor concentrates provided information on the high-purity and ultrahigh-purity products described in this chapter. Articles and product inserts provided information on intermediate-purity clotting factors. The American Red Cross estimate of 1 in 400,000 as the risk of HIV transmission from a blood transfusion was obtained in 1994 from a representative of the Philadelphia branch of the American Red Cross. Articles quoting American Red Cross sources on this risk generally present the same or a similar rate (1 in 500,000).

Dr. Bernard Horowitz spent hours explaining the new virally inactivated "bagged blood" products being developed by Melville Biologics, a subsidiary of the New York Blood Center. He also provided me with a telephone minicourse on viruses.

I obtained information regarding statute-of-limitation issues and the Hemophilia Association of New Jersey's initiative to bring hemophilia-HIV cases to court through my work with that organization's Ad Hoc Legislative Committee and AIDS Task Force. I was present at all events involving this legislative effort: press conferences, committee hearings, full-chamber voting sessions, rallies, and so on. I was also involved in soliciting sponsors and supporters of the bill. I observed the testimony of John P. Sheridan, Jr., of the law firm Riker, Danzig, Sherer, Hyland, and Perretti, lobbyist for Bayer Corporation, during which he described the hemophilia community's fear of discrimination as "disingenuous." Quotations of Sheridan are taken from the written copy of his testimony presented to the New Jersey Senate Judiciary Committee.

Recommendations to the reader regarding the proactive route to solutions are based on my own experiences. Opinions regarding the need for continued and increased vigilance of the nation's blood supply are mine as well as those of the hemophilia community, the Public Health Service, the Institute of Medicine.

The bulk of the information used in this chapter was obtained from published sources and from presentations, including the following:

Adams, Raymond, and Maurice Victor. *Principles of Neurology*, 5th ed. New York: McGraw-Hill, 1993.

Busch, Michael P., et al. "Evaluation of Screened Blood Donations for Human Immunodeficiency Virus Type I Infection by Culture and DNA Amplification of Pooled Cells." *New England Journal of Medicine* 325 (1991): 1–5.

Centers for Disease Control. *Morbidity and Mortality Weekly Report,* July 23, 1993.

Collins, Huntly. "AIDS in U.S. Stabilizing but Still High." *Philadelphia Inquirer,* July 7, 1996.

Créange, A., et al. "Creutzfeldt-Jakob Disease After Liver Transplant." Abstract presented at Seventy-first Annual Meeting of the American Association of Neuropathologists, San Antonio, Texas, June 7–11, 1995.

Dodd, Roger Y. "The Risk of Transfusion-Transmitted Infection." *New England Journal of Medicine* 327 (1992): 419–420.

Evatt, Bruce. "Hepatitis A: Transmission by Blood and Blood Product–Risks of Transmission and Methodology of Surveillance." Abstract presented at the Liver Disease in Hemophilia Conference.

F-D-C Reports. "The Pink Sheet" (a publication of the Food and Drug Administration). January 16, and April 3, 1995.

Finkelstein, Katherine E. "Bad Blood." *New York,* November 25, 1996: 28–37.

Franceschi, S., et al. "Trends in Incidence of AIDS Associated with Transfusion of Blood and Blood Products in Europe and the United States, 1985–1993." *British Medical Journal* 311 (1995): 1534–1536.

Garrett, Laurie. *The Coming Plague: Newly Emerging Diseases in a World Out of Balance.* New York: Farrar, Straus and Giroux, 1994.

Gorbach, Sherwood L., John G. Bartlet, and Neil R. Blacklow. *Infectious Diseases.* Philadelphia: W. B. Saunders, 1992.

Heimberger, N. Von, et al. "Faktor VIII–Konzentrat, hochgereinigt und in Lösung erhitzt" (Factor VIII Concentrate highly purified and heated in solution). *Arzneimittal-Forschung* 31 (1981): 619–622.

Heyman, S. Jody, et al. "How Safe Is Safe Enough? New Infections and the U.S. Blood Supply." *Annals of Internal Medicine* 117, no. 7 (1992): 612–614.

Horowitz, Bernard. "Spectrum of Current and New Viral Inactivation Techniques." Abstract presented at Forty-seventh Annual Meeting of the National Hemophilia Foundation. Philadelphia, October 12–15, 1995.

Horsburgh, C. Robert, et al. "Duration of Human Immunodeficiency Virus Infection Before Detection of Antibody." *Lancet,* September 16, 1989: 637–639.

Jaret, Peter. "Viruses." *National Geographic,* July 1994: 58–91.

Kasper, Carolyn K., et al. "Recent Evolution of Clotting Factor Concentrates for Hemophilia A and B." *Journal of the American Blood Resources Association,* summer 1993: 44–56.

Leveton, Lauren B., et al., eds. *HIV and the Blood Supply: An Analysis of Crisis Decisionmaking.* Washington, D.C.: National Academy Press, 1995.

Lewis, S. M. "How Safe is a Blood Transfusion?" *World Health,* March/April 1995.

Mannucci, Pier. "Efficacy of Current Technologies for Viral Attenuation." Abstract presented at the Liver Disease in Hemophilia Conference.

Meyer, Josh. "Blood-Bank Software Recalled over Defects." *Philadelphia Inquirer,* April 11, 1995.

Nau, J. Y. "CJD and Albumin." *Lancet,* 1995: 442.

Nelson, Kenrad E., et al. "Transmission of Retroviruses from Seronegative Donors by Transfusion During Cardiac Surgery." *Annals of Internal Medicine* 117, no. 7 (1992): 554–559.

Pierce, Glenn F., et al. "The Use of Purified Clotting Factor Concentrates in Hemophilia: Influence of Viral Safety, Cost, and Supply on Therapy." *Journal of American Medical Association* (1989): 3434–3438.

Rock, Andrea. "America's Dangerous Blood Supply." *Money,* May 1994: 135–147.

Scherschmidt, Bruce F. "Hepatitis E: A Virus in Waiting." *Lancet,* August 26, 1995: commentary.

Schiff, Richard. "Transmission of Viral Infections Through Intravenous Immune Globulin." *New England Journal of Medicine* (December 15, 1994), editorial.

Shaw, Donna. "CDC Official Calls for Keen Eye on U.S. Blood." *Philadelphia Inquirer,* November 3, 1995.

Shulman, Stanford T., John P. Phair, and Herbert M. Sommers. *The Biologic and Clinical Basis of Infectious Diseases,* Philadelphia: W. B. Saunders, 1992.

Vrazo, Fawn. "Disease Scare Has Britain in Panic." *Philadelphia Inquirer,* March 22, 1996.

Washburn, Lindy. "Lawsuit Brought by U.S. HIV-Infected Hemophiliacs." *Lancet,* July 8, 1995: 110.

Westfall, Pamela. "Hepatitis, AIDS, and the Blood Product Exemption from Strict Products Liability in California: A Reassessment." *Hastings Law Journal* 37 (1986): 1101–1132.

Wolinsky, Steven M., et al. "Human Immunodeficiency Virus Type I (HIV-I) Infection a Median of Eighteen Months Before a Diagnostic Western Blot." *Annals of Internal Medicine* 111 (1989): 961–972.

ACKNOWLEDGMENTS

My husband, Charles, spent the last twenty-five years trying to persuade me to write a book. I want to thank him for never giving up on me. A quarter of a century is a long time to spend giving encouragement.

While I was writing, my son Erik volunteered to cook for his younger brother, Teddy, and supervise his eating. This was no small task because Teddy's AIDS medications were making him anorectic. Teddy became my library research assistant, which involved, for the most part, searching for and retrieving dusty twenty-pound volumes and reshelving them.

I am embarrassed to admit that despite having a son who is writing his doctoral dissertation in computer architecture, I am nearly computer illiterate. When I bought a new computer and transferred my manuscript from one word-processing program to another, I ran into many problems. I'd panic and telephone Adam day or night, begging for help. He told me that when he answered his telephone and heard sobbing on the line, he knew it was his mother.

There would have been no book without the generous cooperation and encouragement of the hemophilia community. I owe a special debt of gratitude to Elena Bostick, executive director of the Hemophilia Association of New Jersey, for her ever faithful support. I thank especially the many courageous people with hemophilia who telephoned and wrote to disclose the secret of their HIV infection.

I must ask the forgiveness of all people with hemophilia for my use of the word *hemophiliac.* Though I am aware that it is not considered accurate, I couldn't avoid using it. There are only a limited number of creative ways to describe people with hemophilia in a text of this length.

To the many individuals who provided me with an endless source of documentation and to those who sent letters of encouragement, I thank you. One of the most touching letters that I received was sent by a woman in Alabama whom I had never met. She thought of me, and sent a card, on the first anniversary of Cubby's death. I felt the love and compassion of our community surround me as I labored at my computer.

I thank the physicians and scientists who responded to my inquiries, granted interviews, read my rough drafts, and spent hours explaining viruses. Special thanks go to Drs. Bruce Evatt, Don Francis, Bernard Horowitz, Edward Shanbrom, and Thomas Drees.

I appreciated tremendously the court documents made available to me by Eric Weinberg and Tom Mull, two attorneys dedicated to achieving justice for the hemophilia-HIV community. The individual who provided me with the most invaluable help in locating documents is my friend Donna Shaw. She is a woman of admirable integrity. With her access to documents (which she willingly shared), her writing experience, and her connections, she could have easily scooped me on this. She chose not to do so because, as she told me, "You were the one to lose the children. It's your story. I'd be presumptuous to take it away."

I am most grateful to the staff of the Temple University Law Library, Rutgers University Law Library in Camden, and the Library of the University of Medicine and Dentistry of New Jersey, School of Osteopathic Medicine. Without these libraries and the help of their staffs, I could not have done the research for this book. Each and every member of the staff at the National Hemophilia Foundation's

Hemophilia and AIDS/HIV Network for the Dissemination of Information was most gracious about locating information for me. They were tireless and timely in their efforts. Special thanks go to Kathy Crosby, who made me think she was absolutely delighted to drop what she was doing and search for some odd bit of information that I needed immediately.

A special thank you goes to my mother, Yolanda "Lalli" DiGiacomo, who never said no when I called and asked her to listen to a new paragraph or page or chapter. Like a typical mother, she thought every word I wrote was brilliant. Mom waited eagerly for the publication of *Cry Bloody Murder*, so that she could brag. I dare say she would have bored her sisters and friends to tears with it. My mother, from whom I inherited my assertiveness and my bleeding disorder, died of an intracranial hemorrhage just days before I completed the manuscript.

There are three individuals to whom *Cry Bloody Murder* owes its publication: Sharon DeLano, my Random House editor, who courageously took on a first-time book author; Deborah Karl, my agent, whose boldness and savvy were just what I needed in an agent; and my friend Katherine Lamprecht Sabatelli, the high school English teacher who taught me how to write.

To all the members of the hemophilia community infected and affected by AIDS, you often thanked me in advance for serving as your voice. I only hope that through *Cry Bloody Murder*, I have spoken loudly and strongly enough to deserve your gratitude.

INDEX

ABOUT THE AUTHOR

Elaine DePrince serves as chairman of the board and education director for the Cubby and Michael Foundation, a nonprofit health-education organization founded by the author and her husband, Charles. She is an advocate for people with hemophilia and/or AIDS. She lives with her husband and two of her sons, Erik and Teddy, in Cherry Hill, New Jersey.

ABOUT THE TYPE

This book was set in Walbaum, a typeface designed in 1810 by German punch cutter J. E. Walbaum.